River
Journey

Searching for wild beavers
and finding freedom

River Journey

Journey

Searching for wild beavers and finding freedom

BEVIS WATTS

Dedication

To all those who care about the
natural world and our wildlife, and
particularly those who work tirelessly
to protect it and restore what must
once again flourish.

◆Tangent Books

5.16 Paintworks, Bristol BS4 3EH

First published 2022
Second edition 2022

ISBN 978-1-914345-23-4
© Text and photographs Bevis Watts
The Author has asserted his right to be identified as the Author of this
work under the Copyright, Designs and Patents Act 1988

British Library Cataloguing-in-Publication Data:
A catalogue record for this book is available from
The British Library

Book design by Simon Bishop
Edited by Roz Kidman Cox
Typeset in Sabon and Pluto
Printing: Akcent Media

Cover illustration: Pearson Scott Foresman Archives (© public domain)

Contents

Introduction

Europeans Beavers have been extinct in the UK for at least 400 years. While there have been some captive populations on private estates, the first wild beaver reintroductions took place from the early 2000s, initially in Scotland, Kent and Devon and now in an expanding list of locations. In 2020, beavers were released in Cheshire, in Hatchmere Nature Reserve, as part of a five-year plan to restore a valuable wetland system. In 2021, more releases followed, including another pair in the South Downs, two more in an enclosed area in Dorset, an adult and its offspring at Cors Dyfi Nature Reserve in Powys, Wales. Many more releases are on the horizon. Beavers will help enhance these locations in a variety of ways. Some have escaped and established natural populations, and other populations, such as those on the River Otter in Devon, have appeared mysteriously and have, eventually, been allowed to remain. This is a story of another mysterious population, one that is truly wild and free and which has been undetected for some time.

As someone who has been a passionate conservationist all of his life and who has had the privilege of leading one of the Wildlife Trusts earlier in my career, as well as setting up a small conservation charity and volunteering for several others, I have long known of the importance of beavers to a healthy and balanced ecosystem and their significance in supporting a wider range of biodiversity. Indeed, though we are still in the early stages of understanding the depth of their importance to healthy ecosystems,

this is a 'keystone species', meaning that the presence of beavers is of critical importance for the natural environment and biodiversity. They are landscape architects that change their environment to suit their needs and, in doing so, create complex wetland habitats for many other species.

I had wanted for some time to try to visit one of the reintroductions in the hope of seeing beavers. Indeed, a friend had invited me to be her guest on a trip to see the beavers on the River Otter in Devon, but the trip was postponed due to the Covid-19 pandemic lockdowns, and I had yet to make it there. So imagine my delight when I received an email from a Wildlife Trust colleague saying "I'd love to introduce you to some other large furry mammals," implying they were beavers. The 'other' is referring to the fact that for more than a decade I have visited a particular badger sett regularly in spring and summer and donated any decent photographs I managed to take to the Avon Wildlife Trust (AWT/the Trust). I am only a very amateur

wildlife photographer, but I had increased my badger photography in recent years to try to provide resources to support campaigns against the badger cull. The AWT colleague also heard I had planned a month off but couldn't go far due to Covid-19 restrictions. She was hoping I might try to photograph the evidence of beavers along the river and undertake a dawn or dusk survey to try to capture evidence. I replied excitedly, congratulating them on being involved with a new reintroduction, only to receive a reply saying that the beavers were truly wild and free and hadn't been reintroduced by the Wildlife Trusts.

What followed turned into an adventure over several months, searching for signs of beavers along part of a river running through private or farmland and only accessible on water. I would get to see them in the wild, find where they lived and witness their positive impact on the environment – and make discoveries of national significance.

Prologue

The reason that I was taking a month off was to rest and recover from a few years of exceptional hard work, stress and strain as a CEO dealing with the challenges of steering a bank successfully through Brexit and then the pandemic. Brexit was a challenge because Triodos Bank was founded in the Netherlands and operated as one legal entity across five countries within the European Union single market. Brexit changed all that. We had to create a new bank in the UK, apply for a UK banking licence and then go through the high courts to get approval to transfer all of the bank's assets and customer accounts to the new UK-registered company. All in all, it cost the best part of £7 million and consumed my life and the lives of many others for more than two years.

I wasn't a fan of Brexit even before having to do all of this because I don't see how we will resolve the world's largest problems, including climate change, without much greater coordination and the sharing of wealth, rather than increased separation and competition. The pandemic stretched all business leaders, with banks heavily scrutinised on their ability to continue to serve customers through a crisis as well as having to support many people and business customers in difficulty, something I am proud to say my team did with distinction. I read somewhere a great turn of phrase about the pandemic: 'We were all in the same storm but in different boats.' While my challenges were not the greatest compared to many people who lost loved ones or livelihoods, they still took their toll.

Regardless of Brexit and the pandemic, the challenges of running a fast-growing, rapidly changing and successful business are intense, and part of leadership is recognising when you need to recharge so you can continue to give to the cause and to others.

As well as needing physical recovery, I also needed time to reconnect with myself, slow down and find a better balance, with a greater focus on working to live, rather than living to work. That said, I am passionate about what I do professionally, and I also need a strong sense of purpose, as I'm easily bored with the mundane or pointless. So the challenge of trying to gather evidence on the existence of genuinely wild beavers in the local landscape couldn't have been a more perfect focus. I needed restoration of my own landscape and my own rewilding to recover aspects of myself that were in danger of becoming extinct.

A yoga teacher at a retreat I used to attend regularly taught me to see that everything in life is positive and that you need to embrace it as such. It takes some time to reflect and see things in that way, and while I had planned my month off about seven months prior to May 2021, I was not expecting to still have strict pandemic restrictions in place and be unable to travel. But my exhaustion meant that having a completely clear month was a huge positive, as was being single, which meant I had no responsibilities or accountabilities and could embrace any opportunity. It wasn't to be a month submerged underwater scuba diving and finding mindfulness in ways I had become familiar with, but it was an opportunity to intensely submerge in other ways.

I have always been my most relaxed and alive when intimate with nature, whether climbing mountains or glaciers, watching wildlife on foot or from a kayak or through my great love, scuba diving. I have been diving for more than 20 years and have volunteered as a diver to survey and protect coral reefs, to photograph whale sharks for research and to undertake ocean clean-ups. Even when diving as a guilty pleasure, I have donated pictures

to support conservation efforts, most recently those of angel sharks in their last stronghold in the Canary Islands. I've also had the privilege to be part of a survey expedition to tag marine turtles on Barrow Island off northwestern Australia – a World Heritage Site inaccessible to the public and labelled Oz's Madagascar, with more than 20 species of animals found there and nowhere else due to its separation from the mainland for millennia. Despite having to avoid the five species of deadly snake, working on the island through the night tagging turtles in moonlight remains the most memorable experience of my life. It is those sorts of adventures and purpose that I have always sought and which have found me, and the depth of relationships you form both with nature and with your fellow humans through the shared experiences of wildlife and sense of being at one with nature are what give me the greatest fulfilment.

Opportunities for such adventures have become limited as my career and responsibilities have progressed, and I have often found myself a stranded diver. I am something of a tropical fish at heart and haven't dived in the cold waters of the UK for many years, contenting myself with the occasional snorkel or seeking out seal and seabird colonies on land. I am also conscious of the impacts of flying, and a large part of my diving has been done with a purpose while volunteering on conservation programmes or combined with visiting members of a family scattered around the world. But 2020's Covid-19 lockdowns and five-mile travel restrictions taught me to create more of my own adventures. Once they lifted, I had one of my best holidays simply living by the weather and the tides in Devon and kayaking or walking the Axe Estuary and Seaton wetlands. Here I discovered nesting sand martins in the riverbanks, watched spawning sea trout in the stone and shingle shallows and encountered a barn owl swooping silently on its prey. It reminded me of how much opportunity I really had. The only thing I lacked was a selfless purpose beyond my own pleasure and hobbyist photography. What I have learnt about myself is that I prefer intimacy with a place – noticing its changes and understanding its wildlife. The joy of wildlife for me is greatly enhanced when you know where to find something, how to be around it and how to watch it undisturbed.

There was some irony in my new adventure being tracking down beavers. 'Beaver' was a name-calling taunt in my school days. The name Bevis is actually pronounced as in Beverley or beverage (a later nickname – ironic because I have never been a great drinker). In fact, I was named after the character in the book *Bevis: The Story of a Boy*, by nineteenth-century nature-writer Richard Jefferies, in the hope that I would have as good a life as the boy. The tale is one of adventure, exploring the imaginary lands that Bevis creates in the countryside where he lives with his best friend and dog. There are strong moral undertones to Bevis doing the right thing and looking after those less fortunate, and there is also another element to the name – as chosen by my father, who was an evacuee as a young teenager in World War II – because in the book there are no parents, just learning through exploration and adventure, which was probably a contrast to a wartime childhood.

In my adult life, I discovered that the name Bevis arrived in Britain with the Norman invasion of 1066 and is derived from the Norman French 'belfils', meaning 'handsome son'. How I wish I'd known that as a child, to use as a comeback to my taunters. I could also have turned the moniker of 'beaver' into a compliment, proclaiming that I was a keystone species and vital to the health of the ecosystems and life on Earth itself. A greater irony in my new adventure tracking beavers was that, during my time as chief executive (CEO) of AWT, a senior politician of one of the region's councils once remarked to a colleague, "I have been having terrible trouble with the Beaver Watch." My colleague was confused as to what he was referring to until the councillor enlightened them that he was referring to Bevis Watts.

Not through our own choice, AWT had been in a very public dispute with North Somerset Council (NSC), concerning the abolition of a roof tax per house on a new housing development, contracted to be used to fund the management of a nature reserve created by AWT called Portbury Wharf. The reserve was on former ash fields from a coal-fired power station and was widely acclaimed for the wetland habitat created, for the high-tide bird roost and for the successful repopulation of water voles, among other achievements. It was also of national significance because of the funding mechanism whereby each house built would pay an annual levy to maintain the reserve – hailed by DEFRA itself as a model for new developments to enhance the natural environment and protect it in perpetuity.

'The Leader' of NSC (as he insisted on being called) was also a director of a company that collected the roof tax. Without consultation, legal agreements were ripped up excluding AWT from a deal done between the house builder and NSC to abolish the levy and take the reserve under council control. There were two reasons for this, in my opinion. First, upcoming elections with a minority but very vocal group of residents unhappy about the relatively small annual levy they had agreed to pay when purchasing their homes, and second, because on the horizon was the prospect of the Hinkley Point C nuclear power station connection being brought ashore across the nature reserve. Reneging on planning consents, abolishing the levy structure and removing AWT meant a senior NSC cabinet member would be more assured of his seat in the elections and that the council could smooth the way for the Hinkley Point C engineering works, while receiving an estimated £1 million in compensation payments without the Trust's scrutiny. Money from the levy would have also gone to a promised education centre that has never materialised.

We received great support from the local community and media, but couldn't engage anyone at DEFRA to take serious interest, despite the national significance, and didn't have the resources to take on an entrenched legal battle with a major house-builder and a council. The local MP, Dr Liam Fox, made positive noises on the need to protect the reserve but never engaged with the real issue or commented on the actions of his Conservative colleague.

The Leader is now deposed, with the Conservatives having lost control of the council. At the time of writing, as the Hinkley high-voltage connection proceeds as foreseen, Portbury Wharf has a temporary road going through the middle and large trenches. A site for nature that was created in mitigation of the construction of hundreds of homes on the flood plain beside the Severn Estuary saw temporary biodiversity gain before, yet again, another example of nature making way for 'progress', and it will be years in recovery if at all.

In making a strong stand against the NSC's action, we were fighting for a principle. I have worked hard all my career not to politicise myself or the organisations I represent, and at some point, I have had poor experiences in equal measure from politicians of all colours, so I stick to policies and issues. But I take some pride in our struggles reducing a senior politician to name-calling with the 'Beaver Watch'. Years later, while out walking on the Mendip Hills, I would meet a senior council official I respected, who told me that I was right about the motives but that it was a battle we could never have won.

It is ironic then that, several years later, when the fate we foretold of Portbury Wharf Nature Reserve has become reality, my becoming a real 'beaver watch' has also transpired. My lessons from it are that environmentalists and conservationists are too conciliatory and deferential, and if I had my time again, I would have taken more radical action to attract greater media attention – and been more robust on many other issues throughout my career. My successor at AWT was able to play the game of apologising for the row and say AWT was now under new leadership to allow it to engage effectively with NSC on other issues.

For those of us who have been working in sustainability for a long time, these people we are deferential to are getting it wrong too often and the systems are failing us, yet too few are really challenging this. Perhaps it happens to everyone that, as they get longer in the tooth (no beaver pun intended), they get more cynical and outspoken. Outspoken isn't really in my nature, as an introverted, reflective person who looks at things from all angles, but if I had my time again, I would be more vocal, challenge and be less compromising on many issues. The pace of change isn't just too slow, true vision is lacking from all political parties, and the change is not real enough to reverse the direction of travel on so many environmental and societal issues.

The former BBC Radio 4 *Today* Programme and *Mastermind* presenter John Humphries writes in his memoirs of the need to challenge authority repeatedly, using his experience of the Aberfan disaster, where coal spoil heaps collapsed down a hillside, crushing a school and killing the children and teachers inside. He is right. We all have to do it more. I'm not raising Portbury Wharf with any purpose other than as an illustration of the forces conservationists, environmentalists or anyone working to effect change come up against, and I'll share more examples from very local to national level, as my beaver-surveying adventures proved a great time for reflection and clarity. I won't cover much from my time at the bank, in part because this book is a personal work, not a professional one, so it isn't appropriate, particularly when I'm the serving CEO, but also because there are many things you have sight of as a bank manager that you have to take to your grave.

I have been writing and publishing on various aspects of sustainability throughout my career, including in numerous academic journals, international conference proceedings, professional publications, independent blogs and, in recent years, in media outlets such as the Reuters Foundation and the *HuffPost*. I had my first letter published in a national newspaper in 1998, in *The Independent*, where I criticised an article on recycling as missing the point, having only covered the issues of collection and not even mentioned the fact we already had vast oversupplies of many of the collected materials and no viable markets for them in the UK, which undermined the entire economics of recycling. A long-time collaborator, Andy Rees, who for decades has been an inspiring leader on waste and resource issues for the Welsh Government, told me at the time that I came across as an angry young man, which I took to heart but which I now look back on with some pride. It was the start of writing beyond my academic work, and I enjoy the process of writing as it prompts reflection and the creativity of crystallising often complex issues. For the bank, I have been fronting a weekly column in the *Metro* newspaper on 'greening your money', trying to inspire more people to think about what their savings and pensions funds are funding and whether that is aligned to the future they think they are saving and investing for.

All that said, I do not regard myself as a writer, and I started this book just as notes, with no purpose other than to reawaken my creativity and keep my adventures with beavers alive. As time went on, I realised that

I was writing a story of personal experience, as witness to the ecosystems the beavers create and recover and of the impact they had on me. It is that positive story which I wanted to tell, to inspire more to realise that we don't always have to have every piece of evidence for change. Sometimes we have to reconnect with what we inherently know and experience and lead change for the better. It is a story to challenge authority to move faster and to treat the climate and ecological emergencies as emergencies.

An emergency – "something dangerous or serious ... needs fast action in order to avoid harmful results". Cambridge Dictionary

1 The Challenge

It was a beautiful sunny late-April evening when I met my co-conspirator, Amy Coulthard, Avon Wildlife Trust's Director for Nature's Recovery, in Batheaston near Bath. The first swallows were swooping overhead, and I was excited, anticipating a walk around the nearby AWT nature reserve, Bathampton Meadow, on the river Avon. But Amy told me to take my backpack and a drink as we were heading upriver. We walked and talked as we picked up footpaths and zigzagged our way until we reached the riverbank way upriver. So why would a beaver be here instead of the lovely nature reserve? The answer was obvious, willow – a favourite food for beavers. Here there were mature willow trees, some growing partly into the river. As we walked, Amy pointed to the spot where the first signs of a beaver had been noticed. It was a branch about 10 centimetres wide that had been chomped (one of my many technical ecology terms) to a pencil point and some bark stripped from its beam. Then we inspected a much larger tree branch lying flat alongside its fallen but still-living trunk. This branch was much larger at about 25 centimetres in diameter and had been almost completely stripped of its bark, with a large chunk of the branch apparently eaten, crumbs scattered beneath on the muddy riverbank.

This was clearly beaver work, with their teeth marks visible on the bark-stripped wood. But where had they come from? Were the marks left by one just passing through? Has someone illegally started their own private reintroduction? Was it more than one?

So many questions ran through my mind, including whether it was really the work of a beaver, despite there being nothing else that leaves such telltale signs. However, Amy had received a picture taken on CCTV footage from a nearby industrial estate, which showed a beaver complete with its paddle tail walking in the middle of a car park. It was following the Covid-19 social-distancing guidelines along the centre of the pathway but going the wrong way up the one-way system. Apparently, the footage had vindicated one of the workers who, for some considerable time before the beaver made its guest appearance on the CCTV's nightly security alerts, had been the butt of jokes for telling colleagues he had seen a beaver.

Luckily, the business was more perplexed and excited than concerned and had contacted Avon Wildlife Trust. Many might have reacted differently and called pest control or taken action into their own hands. But the beaver had caused no harm and was said to be a source of great curiosity and amusement.

As we continued to walk and talk, Amy shared her vision for working in partnership to help beavers thrive and spread across the landscape, creating habitats for other wildlife and helping nature's recovery in doing so. She wanted to raise funds to survey and monitor the beaver(s) and engage and support the surrounding landowners so they would understand the impact of beavers and support, through adaptation where necessary, the long-term benefits they could bring.

Engagement and advocacy were definitely needed with some of the landowners, all assuming the beaver or beavers had arrived relatively recently and had yet to be discovered. There was also an opportunity for land-use change, with some fields adjacent to the river becoming potential wetlands, adding to the area's natural flood defences.

Amy pointed to a collection of willow branches hanging low into the river on the opposite bank and said that, at first light that morning, colleagues had seen a beaver feeding there. Where bark had been stripped, you could see the freshly exposed white flesh of the tree. This was near to where the By Brook meets the Bristol Avon (the Avon is often known as the Bristol Avon to distinguish it from a number of other rivers of the same name, Avon being a derivative of *afon*, the Welsh for river). There was speculation that the beaver was living up the brook and might have escaped from a private reintroduction at Castle Coombe, which the brook ultimately led to. But what Amy was particularly keen to understand was whether the main activity on the river was just here or if there was activity upstream towards Warleigh Weir. Not far upriver from Warleigh, the Bristol Avon connects to the River Frome, and there was known to be a breeding population established on the Rodden Brook, a tributary of the Frome, though it was not known how beavers had got there, either.

I was happy to try to help solve these mysteries, but I was more excited about the possibility of seeing beavers. I imagine that only a few hundred people at most have seen wild beavers in England, so needed no more persuading to devote some of my time off to the task of trying to get photographic evidence and support the conservation efforts. Amy showed me the recommended field guide on the ecology of beavers so I could school myself on their signs, behaviour and lives, which was purchased the next day. I was now set to become a beaver tracker.

Retiring from the riverbank, we walked inland in a loop back to the Trust's Bathampton Meadow Nature Reserve – only accessible under permit and an inspirational example of habitat creation, achieved over two decades. We dodged nesting Canada geese, admired a sea of cowslips and remarked on how dry and cracked the wetland scrapes were due to a very dry April. Back at the car park, I committed to be on the river with my kayak as soon as time and weather permitted.

But the weather had other plans, and there followed days and then a week of rain, light showers, heavy showers, drizzle, mizzle and even thundering storms. You get the idea. While I am a great believer in the phrase 'there is no such thing as bad weather, just the wrong type of clothing', May ended up being the wettest on record, with twice the normal rainfall for that month. To have a chance of using my camera with good-enough visibility on the water, I ended up watching weather forecasts like a hawk and planning my trips in the windows nature was to provide.

In the time waiting for half-decent weather, Amy walked some of the By Brook and only found evidence on the stretch nearest the main river. So it seemed sensible to focus on the main river. I knew part of the river further up the valley well from walking the footpaths on its banks but had never been on the river. There was a one kilometre stretch past Warleigh that I knew from trying to acquire 80 acres of land as a new nature reserve some years ago, which included that stretch of river and its fishing rights.

The land had some remnant ancient woodland, some interesting grassland species and the potential for an oxbow lake adjacent to the river to provide excellent wildlife habitat and natural flood defences for down-stream Bath. It had been for sale for a while, and I had spent months taking trustees, a council official and others there gaining support. But after I left AWT and the Trust began successfully fundraising, the landowner pulled out of the sale. No reason was given, but the reality is that they probably never expected to sell.

Many people own land and woodlands in particular because of a tax loophole that reduces inheritance-tax liabilities, and while some wealthy people are responsible and indeed seek to promote nature by owning woodlands, many don't care about the land. This particular landowner was on Natural England's radar for not fulfilling their management plans as per the terms of their farming payments and legal obligations within a special area of conservation, and the site had been degrading. Having the land for sale may well have kept Natural England at bay with the assumption they would be able to influence the eventual purchaser. Of course, the landowner most likely never expected anyone to buy a steep-sloping site with a footpath along the river and lower fields that regularly flooded. The agent was furious when they pulled out, and sadly the Trust's vision never transpired.

That land adjoins wider woodland that has been sold off to tax-avoiders and hobbyist woodlanders via woodlands.co.uk, whose business model in part includes attracting interest by dividing woodlands into smaller lots, then selling them at inflated prices. This undermines the landscape-scale approach to conservation advocated by leading conservation groups. The fragmented ownership often means there is no coherent management plan, that the sites are too many and too small for Natural England to oversee and regulate. So the sites fall into neglect or, worse, amateur, poorly informed management.

The pockets of woodland already sold in this area had suffered, with one having several mature trees felled without consent to create a miniature amphitheatre, with various tarpaulins tied to the trees, a shed with a long-drop toilet and various areas of fire-scorched earth. It was appalling. One of the council officials I had walked the area with while trying to sell the vision of the reserve headed back to inform the tree officer about what was occurring. I don't know the outcome, but it would have been a feeble fine and ticking-off at best, assuming they even had time to trace the woodland owner and make contact.

Many other such structural and systemic issues include an agricultural-subsidy regime designed to create over-production and drain the natural environment, a planning regime where compensation payments are too easily frittered away to appease local communities rather than redress the impact on the natural environment, and a national government system that places no value on nature – the very asset we depend on for our clean air, clean water, natural flood defences, crop pollination and more.

These are the real battles in conservation if we are to have any chance of supporting nature's recovery. We can advocate bee-friendly gardening (which I do) and tree-planting, but until we really call out and address systemic issues such as the tax loopholes in land and woodland ownership and give more significant resources to Natural England, a regulator neutered by years of David Cameron's 'greenest government ever' austerity cuts, we are pushing water uphill. The 'con' in conservation, it can be argued, is that for all our efforts and many species and landscape recovery successes, we are currently simply slowing the decline of nature rather than conserving it.

I am an optimist, and I do believe we are seeing a generational shift in values, with young people today far more cognisant of the natural environment and of how their own individual actions relate to it. But the need for education and engagement is still huge.

Among the many human challenges thrown at me as a CEO of a Wildlife Trust were the following: a horse-rider repeatedly cutting locks on gates and threatening colleagues while professing his right to ride in a woodland SSSI (site of special scientific interest), despite there being no bridleway; having to evict travellers from a newly acquired site, which incurred more than £10,000 in costs for the eviction and damages; the mundane issues of fires and bird hides being vandalised or used for antisocial behaviour; and dog-walkers letting their animals roam freely on land that is home to deer, hares, badgers, foxes, weasels and more. Restricting the freedom of dogs may be an affront to many owners, and indeed the odd dog wouldn't be an issue, but everyone thinks their dog is just the odd dog, and dozens of free-running dogs daily have a huge impact on wildlife sites. Oh, and did I mention fly-tipping?

The mind boggles at what issues a beaver-reintroduction programme might encounter, as beavers are often misunderstood, and unless some controls are in place, the potential for conflict with humans is significant. But if there were beavers with a real chance of establishing themselves on this stretch of the Bristol Avon, then I wanted to do everything I could to help them do so and to spread beyond. For the Trust to have any chance of securing funding for monitoring and supporting landowners to avoid conflicts as the beavers spread, firm evidence was needed. I promised to send survey reports and photographs of what I found upriver on my kayak sorties looking for these supersized rodents. Another Trust colleague, Julie Doherty, who was working with Amy, had suggested 'Beaver Watch' as the title. After I told her the story behind that title and not wanting to tarnish the beavers by association, I decided to file my reports entitled 'Beaver Patrol'.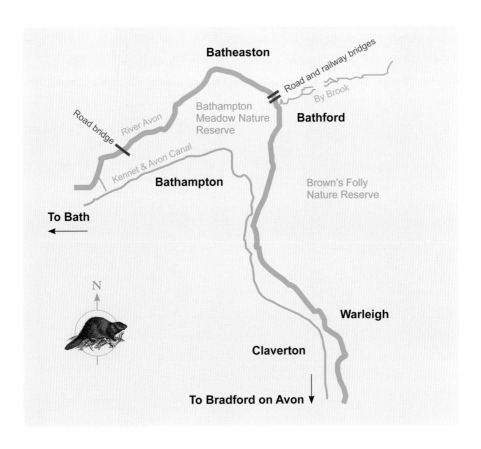

2 Beaver Patrol

Finally the weather improved and I loaded the kayak on the roof of the car, packed my gear and set the alarm for 4am so I would be on the river at first light. I woke to the alarm wondering if this really was such a good idea. The weather may have dried out, but it was cold, and after a quick bowl of granola, I drove off with the car's thermostat showing just 4°C. I arrived surprised to find several cars parked overnight, but the best spot to unload a kayak was free, with a bench next to it to perch kit and camera on. In the half light, I soon discovered that the hazard was goose poo and had to place feet and kit carefully as I got ready to launch. In time, I'd get the packing, loading and unloading drill down to a tee, but this first trip was all a learning curve.

Launching was a challenge because the river level had risen a couple of inches since my recce with Amy, and a submerged block for a sure-foot placement was no longer visible. I had anticipated this, so wore shorts and wetsuit boots and set off wearing several top layers, the thick insulation of my life vest and my favourite warm beanie, binoculars around my neck, my phone camera in easy reach in my thigh pocket and my camera with a weighty 200–500mm lens inserted into the open end of a dry bag and wedged between my legs.

I was wishing I owned a pair of wetsuit gloves, as normal gloves would have been useless once wet from the occasional splash of the paddle strokes, and I was so cold that I was almost wishing I had my full wetsuit on, but

I managed to shut that out to stay focused. I paddled the first stretch of river quite hard, in part to warm up but also because I was keen to get to the riverbank where Amy and I had walked and where a beaver sighting had been previously reported at about 5.30am by another Trust colleague. While I am a strong paddler, this was my first trip of the year, and a hard paddle to warm up meant I was soon thirsty and gasping for the water bottle my 5am brain had left in the car. I am well versed in expedition preparations from the Duke of Edinburgh's Award scheme hikes and camps across Dartmoor in my youth, pan-European cycle trips to raise money for charity, days kayaking on seas and estuaries and weeks living aboard boats at sea on scuba-diving and whale-watching trips throughout most of my adulthood. So, why the hell didn't I bring a flask? This also just showed how out of practice I was and the need to reclaim the balance in my life.

As I went under the road bridge, I forgot about cold and thirst. Ahead, in the arch of the adjacent railway bridge (see page 32), was a beautiful

reflection of the Bathford church tower. The water was like glass, and each paddle stroke broke it crisply. I could see my breath as I exhaled, and there was a mist gathered on parts of the river. It was so eerily silent and still that I felt I was trespassing in another world.

I would spend the next three hours going from Batheaston to near Warleigh and back, zig-zagging the river from bank to bank photographing evidence of beaver activity on my phone. I regularly found stripped bark, cut-off small branches – leaving trade-mark pointed stumps – and part-felled limbs of willow, making them bow at 45 degrees into the water. In hope of a proper picture, I took my camera out of its dry bag and sat it in my lap. I had been reading Derek Gow's book *Bringing Back the Beaver*, and when viewing some impressive beaver tree surgery, I suddenly thought of his stories of being bitten by beavers – one even managing to cut through his pectoral muscle causing a sceptic wound. Alone on the water in half-light, I momentarily questioned what on earth was I doing.

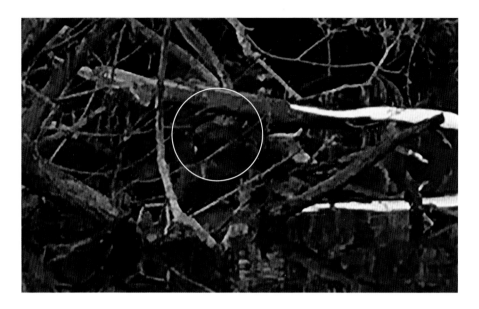

Then at 6.10am, while using my phone to photograph an area of recent activity, thinking it was very recent, I moved around to photograph the next area of activity, when there was a huge *splosh*, like a child dive-bombing a swimming pool, and big ripples emanated out into the river.

Once my heart was back in my chest, I moved to the splosh area, where I found the beaver's abandoned bark breakfast floating towards me. Scooping it up, I put it into the well of the kayak to give to the Trust. Then I thought, hang on, the beaver might have been in the background of the previous area I was photographing. I checked the phone, and amazingly it was. It was blurry but definitely a beaver. I had taken a few frames to compensate for kayak movement and lack of focus, and in one frame it is there, the next it isn't. It was a very poor picture but not bad for a complete fluke, and I would later send it to the Trust with a ring around the hidden beaver. It also showed just how hard to spot well-hidden beavers can be and that getting photographic evidence of their existence was going to be a challenge.

While I only had a blurred image of a beaver, I had gathered lots of images on my phone of bark-stripping and broken but not severed tree trunks and limbs, all of which could support a funding bid by the Trust to explore the beaver's existence further. Now I had a sense of where the beavers were most active, I would go back and leave a camera trap or two.

I emailed a report of what I had found as follows:

Activity
● *There is evidence of feeding activity almost right opposite the Batheaston car park, but there are only a couple of feeding spots that side of the bridge. One of those (I think) has evidence of exiting the river under a chewed willow into a small willow copse on Bathampton Meadow.*
● *There is more activity that you might have thought on the stretch upriver from the bridges, but there is much more activity on the stretch of river after the footpath leaves the field.*

● *Upriver from that field corner, the feeding activity is pretty impressive, with whole tree trunks stripped of their bark and pointed branch stump after stump to be found.*

● *Once you get to an area of the riverbank which is metal railway embankment, then the activity is much less from there to Warleigh. However, there is activity that looks at least a season old and perhaps several years. I was giving up on the embankment to Warleigh stretch when I did find two areas of very recent activity – one of which was the most impressive piece of teeth-work.*

That last find was so ridiculous it made me laugh out loud. Indeed, seeing the change the beavers brought to the river landscape was both fascinating and joyous.

My first assumptions about where beavers might be entering or exiting the river weren't correct, as I'd later witness geese and swans exiting steep riverbanks by walking up them while flapping their wings and leaving a clear pathway with a confusing mix of smudged claw and webbing marks. However, my radar would soon be adjusted.

I would go on to describe and report on the river in four sections to help the Trust follow my path. I had also been told what to look for regarding signs of a beaver's lodge and reported as follows:

● *I saw no sign of a lodge all the way up to Warleigh, although I couldn't do the very last bend, as the river narrows and the flow was too strong to paddle against. I did see what I thought could be the start of one but I think it is most likely to be stripped branches and debris collected at high water, which would be much higher still in winter.*

● *A short distance upriver from where I had seen the beaver (well, a beaver splosh and ripples), there is an area of activity where it is clear the beaver goes up the riverbank and is also feeding on willow bark several metres back*

from the river. The stretch of willow copse goes for a few hundred metres between the river and the railway, and my hunch would be that any lodge would be in there as it is adjacent to the epicentre of activity and it looks as though a bog is fed by water running off from the road/railway and from the river over-topping, as it is the lower riverbank.

I provided the Landranger map grid reference of where I believed the beavers were most likely to live, but the map was too small in scale to show any gap between the railway and river, though there is a five- to ten-metre-wide stretch of willow-laden land for a few hundred metres of riverbank that is inaccessible by foot.

The Trust was delighted with the report and photos of recent beaver activity, and even the blurred beaver image. I wanted to try to get Amy or an ecologist up the river to view what I had found, and I looked into hiring a Canadian canoe, but the weather continued to be wet and the river levels kept rising, making paddling a challenge and making some areas inaccessible safely for an inexperienced paddler. But I was hooked. So I chose not to try to go away during my month off, other than a couple of days here and there, and instead to live by the weather and plan only a few days ahead, aiming to gather photographic evidence by going on beaver patrol in the available weather windows in May – a month that would eventually be confirmed as having twice the normal level of rainfall.

While I wanted to get going again, I was also exhausted after the first survey. The cold and everything being new and needing concentration will have been a factor, but there was also a sense of shallow reserves. I hoped this project would help replenish them, but the first trip was also a wake-up call to listen to my body and pace myself.

A few days later, at just after 5am, I was back on the water for another adventure. I spent a little over three hours looking for new evidence of beaver activity and studying the riverbank for their signs, but I couldn't go as far as last time. After heavy and persistent rain, the river was fast-flowing and a few inches higher than earlier in the week, so it was hard work to paddle through certain parts, and where the river narrowed, I had to paddle hard just to stand still. It confirmed my belief that transporting an ecologist in a Canadian canoe wouldn't be possible for some time.

Amazingly, however, I believe I saw two beavers. As I approached the area where I had taken the blurry phone photo, I paddled very gently, keeping the kayak moving against the flow as quietly as I could. About 30 metres from where I had seen one the other day, and on the same riverbank, I managed to see a beaver before it saw me. It had its back to me – an unmistable furry mass. Sadly, as I raised the camera it shot into the water with a great splash, having spotted me or perhaps heard the sharp intake of breath I made in my excitement. I had got to within

10 metres of the beaver before I had seen it, even though it had been sitting in the open just above the water on a part-sunken branch.

I glanced at my watch, and the time of the sighting was unbelievably exactly the same as my first expedition – 6.10am – and in exactly the same stretch of river opposite a large willow copse, sandwiched between the railway and river. I paddled on so as not to further alarm the beaver, but an hour later, on my return back down the river, I inspected the riverbank more closely for signs of something entering/exiting. It was beginning to look as if this might be the most likely location of a lodge.

I now realised that beavers are, indeed, incredibly hard to spot. I had scanned the area with binoculars before approaching and had only seen the beaver when I had drawn much closer and noticed its movement. Getting photographic evidence really was going to be a challenge. But the Trust needed to know if this was a random beaver or if it was one of a pair or even

a larger population. I thought taking photos of recent teeth marks might help to assess the size of the beaver(s). This could be nonsense, as beavers might use different teeth or techniques that leave different marks. But there were tiny teeth marks on smaller bits of branch debris (see above) and very large teeth marks on the large tree-surgery works (see opposite). I tried using a compass and ruler to measure the teeth marks, but in fast-flowing water, I needed to grip the branch with one hand and take a photo with the other. So in the end, I just used my thumb as a relative measure. I also found a small, freshly stripped branch floating in the river, which I brought back so the AWT team could see the small, quite delicate teeth marks.

Where I could get the kayak parallel to the mud banks, I also looked for paw prints. In several places there were lots of smudged or half prints and the odd claw mark, but I found one clear five-digit print on flat ground facing in the direction of entering the water, which could have been made by a beaver's hind-paw with the digits and webbing unspread. It was inconclusive but was at a spot with two recently stripped sticks. I kept

looking but came to realise that the beaver's large tail is an ideal tool for smudging out their prints and that an array of wildlife used the same mud banks as feeding, cleaning and drinking stations, which meant any print quickly became part of a montage.

Determined to try to solve the mystery of whether there was more than one beaver, I left two remote cameras in the two sighting spots in the hope they might return to these feeding stations. Ducks, passing debris and so on might trigger the camera's sensor and exhaust the batteries and memory quickly, but it was worth a try. To avoid lots of irrelevant daytime shots, I experimented by setting one on a timer from 9pm to 7am. This whole challenge was going to be a process of trial and error, and more errors than successes, with trial and trial again. I paddled homeward with the thought that, though the cameras were relatively inexpensive, they might get spotted and pinched, and that, anyway, if a beaver chewed through the wrong trunk or branch, the cameras would end up at the bottom of the river.

A few days later, a brief weather window enabled me to get out onto the water again. With stealth I approached the section of the river where I had previously seen the beaver. I hugged the right-hand riverbank, staying close to the fringing willows, and paddled as softly as I could whilst still moving forward in the fast flow of the river.

I was moving cautiously and slowly up the riverbank, with the camera ready between my legs, when I heard a splosh some 20 metres ahead, behind a willow jutting out into the river. I saw the ripples and then saw the beaver, heading out into the river and turning towards me. I slowly raised the camera and focused – hard because the light was dim on an overcast morning. But I got a shot before it swam behind a tuft of willow sprouts on a submerged branch. It emerged the other side, facing me. Snap, snap, snap went the shutter, before the beaver saw me and dived with a big tail slap. I could see the near-vertical tail clearly through the viewfinder as it set to slap, but the action was so fast that I had no chance to focus.

I drifted backward on the river, bumping the fringing willows as I checked to see if I had managed to capture a shot of the beaver. I had! Only two snaps were in focus, but I was chuffed. Finally I had the proof that the Trust had been hoping for.

The images showed that the beaver was carrying small branches or sticks (see page 44) and that the first splosh was probably not caused by me. This prompted me to look in the area of the splosh, and hidden behind the willow trunk I could see there was a well-used entrance/exit path and a pile of sticks at the top of the riverbank, which could be part of a lodge. It was awkward to bend over the side of the kayak to take a picture with my phone. But doing so, I could see a second path, though less-frequently used and with indistinguishable paw prints. I was becoming a wildlife detective.

I was convinced that the pile of sticks, with nettles growing on it, was made by the beavers and that it was a well-established but well-hidden entrance/exit. When I reviewed the pictures later that day, I realised there was also a pile of sticks at the bottom of the path. But the beaver had been leaving with sticks in its mouth. So was it starting on a new home? The entrance pathway was located exactly opposite the feeding station where I saw the first beaver and on the willow-copse-covered riverbank that I'd thought would be the most likely location of their home. I was now becoming a student of beavers, and reading my book on the ecology and conservation of the Eurasian beaver, I learnt that, on large rivers, beavers often dig burrows rather than create lodges. That made me more confident that I had found a burrow area, capped with branches and mud, on which the nettles were growing. I also learnt that beavers stockpile winter food caches, which is what the pile of smaller branches at the foot of the riverbank must have been.

I continued upriver and found some new bark-stripping activity and took more pictures. Then some 200 metres from where I had seen the beaver, I heard a large splosh behind me. I looked back over my shoulder to see a beaver swimming towards me. The river was fast-flowing and the kayak started to drift back and naturally turn in the river's flow. Just as the kayak turned, the beaver came within a few metres and then dived with a big tail-slap warning. I had no chance to grab for the camera, needing to keep the kayak stable in the current.

Damn! (No pun intended.) I had been so close, and what a shot it would have been. I must have already passed the beaver without disturbing it when it was spooked by a sheep or other noise on the riverbank. It was about 15 minutes after the first encounter, so a beaver could have easily swum there faster than I could kayak against a strong flow, but I felt it was more likely to be a second beaver because, if it had been the first, it would have been conscious of my presence and unlikely to have been surprised, let alone swim towards me. It was a mystery, and I was starting to second guess and trying to read the minds of beavers.

I decided to paddle as far upriver as I could against the strong current, and then I drifted back at the speed of the river. I arrived back at what I named 'Beaver Alley' (see opposite) after 7am. Assuming the beavers were now in bed, I set about checking the camera traps. The one on a timer had not triggered, though the feeding station it was left on had seen more activity. But I figured the batteries should still be OK for a while and reset it without a timer. The other camera, placed where I had first sighted a beaver, had been triggered but by Canada geese, ducks, a blue kayak and heavy rain. There was a nice little film of some goslings being ushered under and through the willow branches by their parents but nothing else to show for my efforts.

I had realised that paddling to collect the cameras and then paddling back again to put them out was hugely inefficient and also halved the opportunity to capture beaver images, so I had bought two more camera traps and had started to swap them around in ones and twos, depending on which had been triggered. My month off was fast running away from me, but I vowed that, regardless of the weather, I'd swap them at least once more before the end of May. I left one camera tied to an upright branch near the suspected burrow entrance and focused on where the beaver might swim through the willow branches. Placing the cameras was proving harder than I'd thought. Rather than just facing an upright camera in the general direction of a feeding station, I was now trying to find a limb to tie a camera to with the right aspect and angle. There were three cameras in the field, but I still wasn't confident in their placement, as it wasn't possible to look through the viewfinder to check. However, the first phase of my mission – gathering evidence of beavers and an image of one – was complete.

As I headed back that day, content with my success, I saw my first mayfly of the year and felt privileged, given its short lifespan. I had spent three to four hours on each of three trips intensely looking for signs of

beavers and now was starting to appreciate more the wider river landscape and wildlife. As I paddled back, swallows were dive-bombing out of clear blue skies, and as the sunshine warmed the cold morning, I lay back and just drifted, savouring 30 to 40 swallows sweeping and diving the field margins, riverbank and river, one even skimming the surface to take a drink. On the final stretch, a magnificent male bullfinch stared down at me from the branch of a horse chestnut tree, and a female roe deer looked up from its grazing at the top of the riverbank. That deer survive in this fragmented landscape, dissected by roads, railway, canal, river, cycle paths and fences, gave me hope. So much wildlife survives despite our neglect and carelessness. Just imagine what could thrive if we just gave it a little more space and opportunity.

3 Evading capture

While I was exchanging my discoveries with the Trust, I was also keen to share the experience with someone. Getting Amy or Julie upriver in a Canadian canoe was still impossible, given the high river, so I suggested we ask Mark Minkley (see left) to join us. Mark leads the environment team with Bath & North East Somerset Council's planning department and has been a visionary and advocate of lots of positive environmental initiatives. He was one of the close confidants told about the potential presence of beavers, and I also knew he was a keen diver, sailor and kayaker. Mark and I hadn't met up for a few years and it was great to see him, and him being a jammy-bugger meant that we had the warmest day of the year so far and a beautiful sunny evening to paddle upriver – a far cry from my freezing-cold and damp mornings.

We were paddling and chatting up the river, not expecting to see much wildlife in the early evening and laughing at our struggles to pass through some of the fast-flow narrow stretches when, unexpectedly, we saw something swimming across the river about 50 metres ahead. Scrambling for our binoculars, we could see it was a beaver, swimming calmly away from a reed bed, with its tail trailing in the water behind, just as I had seen a beaver swimming towards me on an earlier trip. Beavers are known to emerge at dusk, but this must have been a particularly hungry, early evening diner. We were some way away, and perhaps it didn't see us, as it didn't dive and headed into an area with two dense willows lying in the water.

We looked more closely on the way back and found a large bolt hole in the root-system of a tree – perhaps a regular safe haven. The beaver could not have left the river as the bank is steep-sided, so it must have just let us pass by and then returned to feeding on reeds and other vegetation on the opposite side.

The sighting was about 100 metres upriver from the last point at which you can get on-foot access to the riverbank. In just the two days since my last dawn trip, there had been new activity on a branch on the first section close to the car park and several small new areas of activity near where I had sighted beavers on each trip. We went as far as we could upriver, being unable to paddle fast enough to move against the fast-flowing river. When we turned back, we realised what we had been paddling against for more than an hour, as we returned twice as fast without paddling. Drifting with the flow of the river, I passed Mark a cup of chai tea, and we shared a great moment in the early summer sunshine. Mark briefly bemoaned the lack of cake to wind me up, and we looked forward to some pub grub when we finished.

As we headed back to Beaver Alley, two young guys came ploughing upriver in sports canoes, and we were reminded that, while the beavers were evading capture on my cameras, we also needed to evade the interests of other humans. I checked the remote cameras (see opposite) to find one not triggered, one full with 200 photos or video clips – swans, geese and mostly high-wind and rain movement – and a third featuring several different kayaks and canoes. Still believing it was a numbers game, and that I would be lucky eventually, I left two camera traps, to be rotated in the coming weeks. Mark took phone pictures of me placing them, to help create a visual narrative for the Trust's funding bid, and as it was a nice evening, and the willow-fringed riverbanks looked so beautiful and mystical, I took more scenic shots of the river.

We chatted about the scale of activity and what Mark thought of it all. We both felt that some of the chewed wood was so seasoned that the marks

must be at least a year or two old, which meant that the beaver(s) had been there undetected for some time. Mark had also first paddled that stretch of river 15 years before and many times since, and he didn't feel the beaver(s) had adversely changed it. The character of the river has always been trees lying in the water and blocking sections of riverbank with submerged branches. I could see Mark's visionary mind working on opportunities to change fields into nature reserves and use the beavers' presence to create new wetland habitat, with the flood management, biodiversity gain and tourism benefits that would bring. He said he would find out about the ownership of the farms and fields that run along the river, particularly those that connect all the way upriver to where the beaver(s) live. Our trip ended with the inspiration of countless swifts screeching and feeding in the skies above those fields.

More bad weather frustrated my efforts to get back on the river at dawn, and when a week later my fifth trip eventually happened, the river was higher than it had ever been and I couldn't even travel up two thirds of the river that I had done before. It was like a kayak treadmill. I could see some minor areas of new activity in close proximity to where I believed the burrow to be but none further downriver, which suggested the beaver(s) were staying closer to home. Neither did I hear or see one. I had reached the same area where I had previously seen one at 6.10am, but that was on an overcast morning, and today was a bright sunny one, with the sun coming over the Brown's Folly escarpment at 6.20am. Perhaps when it is so light, the beavers head to bed early, and the very fast-flowing river keeps their feeding activity closer to home. From my experience tagging turtles I knew that moon cycles can influence animal behaviour, and it could be that beavers have some cycles and routines we are yet to understand.

Worse still, the remote cameras didn't deliver a beaver. Again there were lots of shots of paddleboarders coming from Warleigh Weir, kayaks and a small motor launch as well as geese, swans and ducks, and yet more wind shaking. To give some flexibility to where I could place cameras, I had brought a four-foot post with a camera tied to it to stick into the muddy bank or riverbed. Despite discovering that the river depth fell sharply away from the bank and that I could have done with a longer post, I still managed to place the camera looking across to the entrance/exit point where I suspected there was a burrow.

My beaver-study reading continued, and I learnt that beavers typically have a territorial range three to four kilometres long – matching the length of river that I was observing. I also deduced from pictures in the field handbook and online images that the pile of sticks at the side of the entrance/exit point was indeed likely to be the remains of a winter food cache.

I sent in my latest report and insights and got a reply from the Trust saying its first funding bid hadn't been successful but it would be trying again immediately. That first bid had been relatively simple, asking a private foundation for £90,000 for a two-year survey and landowner-engagement programme to monitor the beavers and ensure they could spread safely and without creating problems for humans, particularly farmers.

So much effort goes into raising funding for conservation that it makes the whole endeavour very inefficient, uncertain and high-risk. I have also been on the grant-awarding side when working for WRAP, and learnt that giving money away so it creates real and measurable impact is hard to do well, as you need to secure certain outcomes and satisfy yourself of the robustness of the organisation and that it can deliver. That said, the conservation-funding landscape in the UK needs an overhaul. The various large funders capable of giving awards of hundreds of thousands or millions often require far too much in return for just an indication of interest, draining charitable resources in the process. Earlier, lighter-touch screening and more feasibility grants to develop bids would avoid charities having to invest huge amounts of time and effort into bids that, if unsuccessful, can be detrimental and destabilising.

My vision would be to have multiple funders agree to use the same screening process so there is a common view of national funding priorities, and projects aren't bidding to the same funders in parallel. This requires a much more unified and less egotistical approach. While monitoring and evaluation of awards is important, most funders dominate and control all the communications around projects rather than being truly supportive enablers, and the funder or award of funding often becomes the story/announcement itself.

Even the government needs to look at itself and how it awards funding. Take for example the Trust's project to survey endangered native white-clawed crayfish – a priority species needing protection from predation by larger non-native species, which have escaped from crayfish farms and spread infections that our native crayfish have no immunity to. AWT had hosted the project for the whole of the Southwest for several years, and yet six months into a new two-year funding period, the government body responsible had said it wouldn't be able to fulfil its commitments. As a result, the project ceased and the project officer was made redundant.

The officials were stunned. How could we stop, why? They took no responsibility and ultimately ended up funding continued survey and relocation work delivered through a consultancy, which must have cost them much more. Rant over. But it is yet another example of our systems not being fit for purpose and not joined up in what they are trying to achieve. Don't even get me started on funding for environmental education, which in my view is more competitive than banking and leads to a disparate range of approaches, when what we need nationwide is consistent, high-quality environmental education.

Did I mention my month off had been the wettest May on record? Well, as it came to a close, the weather finally turned, and I went to visit my mother in Devon and paddle the Axe Estuary – from Axmouth up through the Seaton Wetlands and Colyford Common – which boasts fantastic wildlife. Whenever I visit, if the tides are right, I try to paddle in the early morning or at sunset. This time, I was able to paddle late one evening and savoured the rare opportunity. But at the same time my thoughts were with the Bristol Avon and my wild beaver friends. Knowing that, once back at work, I wouldn't have the time to go whenever the weather suited, I headed home early, determined to make at least one more trip before Monday.

On the way back, I stopped to visit a former colleague and friend, Simon Brenman and his wife Chris, who own a 10-acre smallholding on which they have been creating various wildlife habitats. In roasting sunshine, we walked their meadows and new tree plantation – done with the support of Devon Wildlife Trust to try to increase tree cover before the ravages of ash dieback disease really take hold. Recently, they'd had a digger drag out large clumps of reeds that were clogging their tennis-court-sized pond, but a lot of debris from the excavation was littering the surface. We realised the solution was on the roof of my car, and before long, the kayak was deployed like a Thunderbirds mission. I got into the pond to show Simon how to get in and out of the kayak and did a first haul of debris, noticing that the water was alive with literally hundreds if not thousands of tadpoles. We unloaded the floating reeds, roots and general detritus from the kayak, leaving it all close to the water so any wildlife could return. When I got out of the kayak to let Simon in, I realised the water inside contained a palmate newt, lots of tiny shrimps, some tadpoles, a water boatman and several leeches. The captives were given their freedom, and Simon set off on the first of several sweeps to clear up this precious little wildlife haven. This unexpected experience of so much aquatic life just added fuel to my desire to be back on the river.

The forecast for Sunday was for a clear blue sky, and I was primed and ready for the dawn paddle. The water levels had dropped slightly, but the flow was still fairly strong. Once on the water, I was greeted by a dense fog. On my first-ever trip, the fog had been in patches, but this was now along the entire river. It transformed it into a landscape out of Tolkein's *Lord of the Rings*, and as I paddled, I expected elves with bows drawn to emerge on the banks. It was a magical otherworld, but how on earth would

I see any beavers when I couldn't even see 10 metres ahead? Nevertheless, paddle on I did. Then up ahead I saw something moving in the water. Through binoculars, I caught a glimpse of a little face and then clear sight of a head ducking, body curving and a tucked tail smoothly gliding, vanishing into the depths with barely a ripple. Wow! An otter. This was a real treat and bucket-list 'tick', albeit a brief encounter.

Having seen an otter dive, I would now never confuse one with a beaver. The otter moves as one with the water, whereas the beaver has a more chaotic movement, with its unsubtle 'dive bombing' water entries, tail slaps and cumbersome dives – the difference between a stealthy predator and a plant-eater. I had read in Jim Crumley's wonderful book *Nature's Architect* that otters are believed to predate beaver kits, a thought I put out of my mind in the hope that, should any kits be around, the river had enough fish, including the otter's favourite – eels – to avoid temptation.

As I carried on in the fog, a large bird crossed the river at tree-top height. A bird of prey? No, wait, a barn owl! It let out a single, subtle-but-screeching hoot as it headed home, pleasingly in the direction of the escarpment of another nature reserve that the Trust is responsible for, Brown's Folly. With its large, distinctively semi-circular wings flapping, and with the moon still in the dawn sky, the sight was majestic.

Despite many challenges, the Trust has done a great job at Brown's Folly improving the woodland and restoring the limestone grasslands of this Special Area of Conservation. Sadly, in the few years I was CEO of the Trust, some of the reserve's rare-breed grazing sheep were mutilated and killed by dogs. Mountain bikers used the footpaths and areas of the woodland that should be protected. And people broke into a gated network of caves and old mine shafts to host raves in what is the underground hibernation site for a large proportion of an estimated 15 per cent of the UK's greater horseshoe bat population that lives within the reserve and surrounding conservation area. It always comes down to education and awareness.

If people really knew what was there and what they were jeopardising, I am sure they would respect these places more. However, such issues remain the realities of conservation land management and, all too often, a distraction from the job of restoring the natural landscape.

As the sun rose, I suddenly felt its heat on my back and turned to see it breaking through the trees with a burning orange glow and visibly start lifting the fog on the water (see page 58). Perhaps, not surprisingly in these conditions, I didn't see a beaver or much in the way of birdlife, either. However, I retrieved the camera traps, and when I got home, realised one of the cameras had finally caught a beaver. This was the camera I had placed at the entry/exit point to the possible burrow, but I hadn't positioned the post correctly, so the night-vision shot of the beaver about to enter the water was only a partial one – of most of its head, its ears and half its back (see page 60). It was just one individual, so I was no closer to solving the mystery of whether there was a breeding group. I needed to have faced the camera downward more and allowed a greater distance between it and its likely subject, as the lens has a limited wide angle of view. But it did feel something of a triumph, and I proudly sent it off to my Trust colleagues saying "see bottom right corner of the attached". I had to bring the camera back to recharge, but I was already planning better shots, being well into the journey of camera-trap trial-and-error learning. My challenge now would be that, due to work and the importance of weekend rest, I would probably be limited mostly to evenings when the weather cooperated.

The fog lifted at 5.50am as the sun hit the riverbank, which again made me wonder if beavers go to bed earlier once their lodge area is in full sunlight. I hadn't seen any new bark/tree activity on the first stretches of river, so it still appeared that the beaver(s) were staying closer to home than a few weeks ago. There were some new signs of small branches being eaten in the vicinity of the burrow, and some small area of bark-stripping further upriver, where I could partly paddle, now that the strength of the river's flow had slightly subsided.

However, in general, there had been very little new activity, despite the time that had lapsed between my trips. So perhaps the beaver was diversifying its diet from willow bark, given the abundance of willow shoots and other vegetation now available, with the warmer temperatures leading to a late explosion of spring growth.

Going through the images and film clips from the camera traps, I realised just how much the habitat created by beavers is used by other animals. The water around the fallen willow is calmer, and this and other calmer suburbs around the low-lying tree limbs and river debris that gathers around them would also create hiding, feeding and resting places. I got clips of ducks and geese gathering/hiding their young in among the submerged and low-lying branches, a heron fishing in the calmer, clear waters, and swans feeding on the dense roots springing from the sunken willow and the algae and vegetation that they then support. I had also captured lots of different birds perching, drinking and bathing. In the background of a film of a male mallard coming to rest on a submerged branch was a fish lunging for a mayfly, which had escaped to the shallow right next to the riverbank. The beaver's role in habitat creation and its reputation as a keystone species in nature's restoration was evident beyond anything I would ever have imagined when setting out the camera traps within the beaver's aquatic world.

If only I could take and show other people what I was seeing. The epilogue of Derek Gow's book is a hugely uplifting and emotive description of the flora and fauna that the beavers have restored to the landscape following their reintroduction in Devon. Such projects are so important in building the evidence base. That said, I have at various times in my career been frustrated by the need for evidence seeming to override common sense. For example, when trying to get GP surgeries to prescribe time, exercise or therapeutic treatments in nature as prescriptions to help treat conditions such as obesity, anxiety and depression, as well as underlying issues such as social isolation. The Wildlife Trusts had to secure grant-funding to run multi-year trials, with independent evaluation by a university, just to get some pilot prescriptions (and thus paid time) to help people reconnect and rehabilitate in nature. This was despite a local water company advocating non-drug treatments for such conditions, having monitored the increase of many drugs such as statins that need to be removed in waste-water treatment processes. (It also had some great stories about the spikes it would see in recreational-drug deposits on certain nights of the week.)

Anyway, our mental health as a society is poorer because of an increasing disconnect from nature, and many physical conditions could be addressed by being more active outdoors in nature. Indeed, funding people to be supported in this way could also help care for and restore our green spaces and replenish biodiversity. This frustration is, to my mind, rooted in a lack

of leadership through common sense. Too many politicians, leaders in the health sector and civil service fail to act on what they know to be true, living in fear of following common sense without watertight evidence. It is easier to maintain a paradigm we know isn't right than take responsibility for change that we inherently know is right. We have repeatedly damaged the natural environment and public health, and continue to do so, even when the evidence is there, for example, the policies on the use of neonicotinoid pesticides and the badger cull, which fly in the face of the scientific evidence.

Luckily, in the case of that photo of the part-beaver, I had remembered to set the clock on the camera (my dawn brain forgot almost every time), and I noted that it was taken at 9.19pm. So that might be an indication of when it, or they, normally emerge, compared to the early evening diner that Mark and I encountered some weeks before. The idea took hold of being on the water late one sunny summer evening, or mooring on the opposite

riverbank to try to photograph them, if the Trust ever succeeded in starting a landowner-engagement programme that permitted access.

I hoped I'd be able to continue to rotate the camera traps, even if less able to visit at dawn. I had become more accustomed to the 4am alarm clock, and adaptation, along with the time off, had meant my energy was improving and the days of being exhausted and able to do nothing were behind me. I was, in fact, waking up earlier most mornings and had the energy to get the occasional 10-mile bike ride in before breakfast. But there was anxiety about how much I could sustain my beaver-watching while working, yet knowing that doing so was critical to rekindling the creative and adventurous flow that had almost become extinct in me. The beaver(s) had still evaded photographic capture, and I figured that as long as I always left a camera trap out in the field, I would have to go back.

4 Wildlife bringing balance

Was it going to be realistic to be kayaking at dawn on weekends or even in the evenings alongside a high-pressured and demanding job? Weekends were important recovery time from 50- to 60-hour weeks. Driving to the river at dawn took 30 minutes (versus an unpredictable 45 minutes later in the day), and though parking was always assured, packing/unpacking and paddling six to seven kilometres did take a lot out of me. However, the draw of wild discoveries was too great, and with the weather looking set fair, I decided to go again on the Sunday after my first week back in the office.

I also committed to write about my beaver adventures. There was no purpose behind this other than not having had, of late, an outlet for my creativity, and I have always enjoyed writing, though nowadays I only produce occasional thought-leadership articles for work or board papers. I decided I'd write more about not just the trips but the whole opportunity these wild beavers had created for me and how their recovery in the wild was also supporting something of a recovery and renaissance in me. Writing was a commitment to myself to keep this wild project and the balance it provided alive.

I had spent a month being able to choose weather windows, and now with my time limited, I didn't have that luxury. The forecast the night before was not encouraging, but I packed the kayak, cameras and gear and decided to wake at 4am to see what the weather had in store. At first light it hadn't rained, so I headed off, eager to get back on the river. As I was driving there, raindrops started to splatter the windscreen, but I wasn't going to turn back.

I arrived to find, to my affront, that my usual parking spot was taken. A white VW Transporter van occupied the prime spot, with a paddleboard visibly poking into the front seats, shorts and a rash vest hanging on a wing mirror and blue swim shoes set out to dry on the bench. I assumed someone was sleeping inside and went about my preparations quietly but took the adjacent bay to still have a little help from the high kerb in offloading and loading the kayak. The air was damp and oxygenated, the kind that automatically makes you take a deep breath and fill your lungs and savour the scent of spring.

The river level had dropped considerably after a week of hot, dry weather, and boarding the kayak was more awkward than usual, but I was underway and on calm, slow water that was barely moving, with only the smattering of catkins on the surface revealing the steady progress of this calm stretch. There is always something about those first, soft paddle stokes – elation at the start of an adventure and a sense of strength and control as your fresh arm and shoulder muscles move the kayak along with ease.

Only a short way up the river, a thin mizzle was in the air and wetting my head. It was so light that it did not affect the glasslike surface of the river, and reaching back into the pocket of my kayak seat, I pulled out my cap and ventured on. This first stretch of river had generally been quiet, and I usually focused on getting into my paddle stroke and breathing in the dawn air before giving any serious thought to wildlife encounters. However, only a short distance into my paddle, I heard a great spotted woodpecker pecking a tree on the riverbank by the Bathampton Meadow nature reserve. It was right above me somewhere, but I couldn't catch sight of it and was then distracted by a splash along the steep riverbank 30 metres ahead. I made a few soft paddle strokes and peered through my binoculars. I assumed it was

a duck or moorhen having a morning bath and took another few gentle strokes forward to see two otters dive towards mid-river, perfectly synchronised. I could clearly see the curve of their backs and tucked long tails as they dived, with just a clean, single ripple ring as their trace. Then there was a little splash from the same place and I realised there was yet another otter – a smaller one, a young one – no, two!

My camera was still in the dry bag, protecting it from the mizzle. Quietly, I unclipped the bag and withdrew the camera, and as I did so, an adult returned, causing the young ones to splash some more. It was bringing food to them, and when it disappeared again, the two pups splashed some more, seemingly in a playful fight. This was all happening just 10 metres from my floating not-so-hidden hide. I was desperately trying to focus the camera in a very dark area of river, with large trees overhanging and the kayak slowly drifting backward and away. All I managed were a few poor shots before an adult must have sensed my presence and, with some inaudible form of communication, ushered the young away. I could see a few air bubbles surfacing upriver and waited a moment before paddling on. The illusive woodpecker had moved tree to join me and hammered away above, seemingly celebrating in my photographic torment.

I didn't inspect the spot where the otters had been until my return journey, when just below the surface I could clearly see a natural shelf formed by the roots of a large horse chestnut tree, like a step into a swimming pool. Approaching the bridge, I could see in its shadow on the other side more large but calm ripple rings, no doubt the otters moving on as they realised I was continuing upriver. That was the last sign of the family and proof that even a young novice otter is in complete control of when you get to see it. If only I could have let them know I was a safe friend.

The surface of the river was alive with flies and other insects. I had usually experienced this on my return journeys as the sun came up, but on this warm, damp morning, at just 5.30am, the glassy surface was teaming with life. The occasional jumping fish taking advantage of the abundance of insects was all I saw for a while until I came across some spectacular new beaver activity. A willow tree, part-eaten, lay deep in the water. The sheer carnage the beaver had caused made me smile: a thick tree chomped through at the base, with just enough left for it to hang onto life. Its freshly stripped trunk and branches were golden, and I took photos of this new find. As I turned the kayak and made my first strokes upriver, there was a large belly-flop sound from willow 20 metres or so up the river – definitely not my slinky, almost silent otter friends. At this point I realised that I needed to retrain my brain. Instead of getting excited by new beaver-activity finds and becoming fixated with their beautiful fresh colours and texture, I needed to think 'this appears fresh, look for the beaver'.

It was 5.58am when I heard the splosh in the exact same spot on the river where Mark and I had seen a beaver on our evening paddle, some

400 metres from Beaver Alley. I paddled on and upped a heron from reeds in the centre of the river. The heron is often there, and again I reminded myself to think ahead and not just about beavers. It would be the first of six encounters with the heron that day. Each time it took flight as I got within range and raised the camera. I was mid-river looking towards the remote camera I had left at one of the apparent entry/exit points when there was another large splosh a short distance ahead – from the same place I had my first-ever encounter with a beaver.

I sat motionless except for the slight drifting of the kayak. Then there was another splosh behind me, but a little different – like when you first haul yourself out of a pool after a swim and the water rushes off you. It came from the area I had identified as a beaver main entry/exit and potential burrow. Suddenly, right next to me, a beaver popped up. It was facing away towards the previous noise and then dived with a huge tail slap that made me jump and created a small wave that momentarily rocked the kayak. It was warning others and sending me a clearly audible message, the first part of which I won't repeat and the second part of which was 'off!'

Surely there were two beavers? Had the one that made the first belly-flop swum towards and under me while heading for the safety of home? Surely it couldn't have made all three sploshes in such a short space of time, and if it had made the second, why would it come back into mid-river when it was already home? Unless this was a clever beaver creating an illusion, there had to be more than one, but I had not heard them far enough apart on the river to have absolutely no doubt. All of this had happened just after 6.10am, and I wondered if perhaps they were still up today because it was overcast and dank.

The lower water levels and slower flow of the river meant I could now cover the same length I had on my first paddle a month earlier. However, the growth of the vegetation in the form of reeds and new shoots on the sunken trees did force the water into some faster-flowing central channels and created new challenges. I found some more new beaver activity at one of the farthest points, after which I turned and headed back. I wondered if some of the outlying activity was a beaver marking its territory, as it seemed a long way to swim for a snack. Beavers mark their territory using anal-gland secretions – castoreum – the scent of which apparently conveys information such as gender and kinship and probably an individual's signature. As I drifted back with the flow of the river, supping ginger tea from my flask – and missing the heron portrait several times – I also noticed that one of the bark-stripped trees was not a willow but an aspen, which is rare on the river but clearly another favoured beaver food.

It was an hour after my sightings in Beaver Alley when I returned to attend to the camera traps, aware I had not yet seen the beaver on my return leg. I was hopeful about what the camera might reveal, only to get them home, download them and find a squirrel and a domestic cat's tail were the sum of it. My photo collection of wood pigeon, blackbird, magpie and grey heron (got you at last!) also grew.

Placing the cameras was now more of a challenge, as the lower water levels meant I couldn't get near the water's edge around where the beavers lived due to previously submerged branches now being exposed. I got the camera on the post as close as I could, but frustratingly not in the place where I had captured a part-image. I wrestled with a few locations, and I also tried the area of fresh activity on the way back, but when I nearly capsized trying to tie a camera in the only feasible place, I had to admit defeat, vowing to visit the garden centre for some longer wooden posts before my next trip. Even just a metre or so away from the riverbank, the four-foot posts simply disappeared into the soft mud of the river bottom and sank below the water, such was the river's steep and deep topography.

Having had an amazing morning, I now paddled speedily back, but as I came to the spot where I had last seen the otter, I paused to drift and packed away the camera, as it had got wet enough in the intermittent light

drizzle. Drifting under the bridge, there was a perfect view of a beautiful kingfisher looking back at me on its perch. Typical! As I drifted closer, it moved perch 10 metres ahead, giving me a chance to take the camera out of the drybag, but as I took aim, it flew to a higher perch and then behind me. That woodpecker was laughing somewhere!

I am ashamed to say that I polluted the river for the first time that day. I believe in leaving nature as you found it. I won't trample over woodlands or meadows just to get a picture, preferring to work with what I can from the paths and fringes. And on my previous trips, I had collected cans and plastic bottles from the river. But this time I realised my camera lens cap was missing. I can only presume I didn't place it in the dry bag when taking it off quickly to try to photograph the otters.

The guilt of such things stays with me, and on future trips, in penance, I would collect every bit of litter I could find.

As I got out of the river, I found a paddleboard instructor preparing a novice student, the buzz of an electric air pump sounding out across the car park, with no concern for the sleeping inhabitants of the VW van. Energised by my otter and beaver encounters, I packed speedily and by 9am was home. After spending three of the first five hours of the day on the water seeing some incredible wildlife, I was so spirited that, after a second breakfast of sourdough toast, juice and some fruit, I was furiously typing up this story of the day. That moment was the start of this book, as I sat and streamed off 3,000 words. I didn't start writing with any idea of why or an outcome. Rather, it was a way of keeping my time on the river alive and reflecting on what the beavers' restoration in the landscape was doing for my own restoration.

As if I wasn't hooked already on the challenge, I certainly was now. Wildlife has always been a passion, but beavers have turned into something of an addiction, and I was enjoying more than ever sharing pictures and tales with those in the know, as it kept the excitement alive. It also made me want to return at every opportunity. Maybe I could make a weekend dawn trip each week, certainly in the summer months, when the warm temperatures and slower flow of the river make the whole thing less physically exerting. My mind and body would let me know in the days and weeks ahead.

Having seen a film about the US author J D Salinger, I took away the idea that if you want to write, you need to make space for it and do it for at least 15 minutes a day. For a time that worked, often drawing me in to write for longer, and even when it didn't, it focused my determination and appetite to write more comprehensively at weekends. In writing I was also exploring and connecting with my thoughts and feelings.

A month off was some recovery from a brutal few years but not enough. Perhaps getting up at 4am to kayak 6–7 kilometres is a bit extreme, but it is the sort of immersive and physically tiring distraction I need to relax. I love scuba diving because of the wildlife but also because of the concentration required and the complete immersion in another world that serves as a counter-balance and switches off an intense mind. The kayak expeditions were not the same, but after a paddle, when I don't feel I have to do anything but relax and have extra cups of herbal tea, those hours are heaven.

The photography is important, not because I have aspirations (or delusions) about being a wildlife photographer but because it provides a way to share the experience and bring it alive again when discussing with friends or colleagues. I've read and heard about the importance of reminiscence in supporting people with dementia, but I think it can support mental health generally, and certainly the pictures I have taken over the years when scuba diving or wildlife-watching are moments I can return to at an instant, such is the vivid impression they leave on my memory.

The beavers were bringing me an intense focus and purpose. When I wasn't on the river, sorting and sharing photographs or starting to write, I was preparing kit and musing on the challenges of the remote cameras. I'd had several rotations of the cameras now and tried different locations for both feeding stations and riverbank entry/exit points. Aside from finding suitable branches to tie them to and the posts being too short for the depth of the river, there was the problem that, if you faced the cameras out into the river, you might capture a wealth of passing wildlife but only the top of the head of a swimming beaver. If you faced a camera looking along the riverbank, it would often be set off by vegetation blowing in the wind, and you needed just the right angle for the beaver to trigger the trap at a good-enough focal length. What I needed was a placement a little way into the river but close to the bank so as to face the entry point and capture any movement up and down the pathway. I was truly immersed in this wildlife challenge and finding more balance in myself in the process.

5 Expect the unexpected

It was the hottest day of the year so far, and at 5am I was greeted by clear blue skies, though there was a thin mist on the low-lying fields and river. The light and heat must have had some locals up early as, when setting up, I saw one for the first time – a grumpy fellow who didn't wave back as I set out on the river, glad to be back in this peaceful idyll. Many hot, dry days meant the river level was the lowest I had seen it. Although the sun was yet to hit the river valley, it had been up for some time, and in my experience, these clear, bright conditions make for less wildlife activity. As I headed upriver, I saw no wildlife of note except the grey heron rising in the mist and heading off further upriver. However, a short distance along, it emerged high on a perch, gleaming in the first beams of sunlight to hit the river – a majestic sight in the blue-grey misted valley (see page 2).

Reaching the spot where, on my last trip, I had discovered the beaver-felled willow, I found further bark-stripping and small branches bitten off. Seeing no other new activity, I just floated on the water, listening to the birdsong. It was then that a sports canoeist passed me coming up the river. I remarked on the beauty of the morning, then turned back, intent on setting the camera traps before he returned. The river was so much more accessible now and the weather perfect, but I was still a little surprised to see that someone else had set off shortly after me so early in the morning. It raised a thought about the beavers being noticed over the summer if more people started using the river in the early morning and late evening.

Earlier, when approaching Beaver Alley, where I believed the beaver(s) lived, there had been a large entry splosh, followed by a tail slap almost parallel with me. The beaver had come from an overhang of willow, so there is no way I could have spotted it, and I presumed that it had headed underwater, the short distance across the riverbark to home. By now, it would have gone to ground for the day. So on returning there, I set about putting out the refreshed camera traps. The first was placed purely speculatively on a tree trunk overlooking a willow bough in the water, which had an aged area of stripped bark but plenty more to be eaten and new shoots. If I ever managed to predict where the beaver feasted, I'll give up work and lead tours for photographers, I thought, but knowing my luck, the beaver would fell the trunk I had tied the camera to.

The other two cameras were on posts, and one was placed looking along at what I believed to be a riverbank entrance to the beaver's home. I presumed that it climbed out of the water on the branches and then crossed through the network to the muddy tunnel entrance, now visible because of the fall in the river level. The fact that the entrance would have been underwater is why the remote cameras had proved so unsuccessful. Gazing through the mass of living willow branches, I could only partly see it, and sticks covered the top. I speculated that the beavers only occasionally use the other entrance that I thought was the main one. However, this was largely about making myself feel better for the failure so far to get any decent pictures, let alone my ultimate ambition of trying to establish whether a single beaver or a family lived here. While I had seen beavers on all except one trip, I had only once sighted a beaver before it saw me and therefore only once had any chance of a shot.

The final remote camera was on a new six-foot post. Even though the post was less than two metres from the riverbank, the camera strapped to the top sat just above the water, indicating that the central riverbed must be truly very deep. It had been a nightmare to place, and I hadn't got it exactly where I wanted it, so if the beaver had used only the left side of the track to enter/exit, I'd have missed it. I struggled replacing the camera because the lower water level meant I couldn't kayak into the willow as I had done before. With one leg in the water, I had to part-float and part-drag the kayak as close in as I could, reaching down to pull forward or push down on the submerged branches just below the surface. Even then I part-flooded the kayak as I tipped forward, trying to get enough downward force on the post. As I pushed my way back out of the sprawling willow, I realised that, with more fine weather forecasted, the river level would surely fall further and I'd have to get the camera after rains or come ready to swim and clamber over the submerged willow copse.

With a wet backside, I collected the remote camera I had out in the river. As I glanced through the images, I realised it had been tampered with. That the cameras would be found had always been a possibility, but despite all the human activity captured on previous footage, this was the first time. A paddleboard was in one frame and, before that, blurry shots of the riverbank. So they had obviously handled it and then put it back, though not in the right place.

A little uncomfortable from my wet clothes, I paddled back steadily, just as the sun lifted away the mist and the surface came alive with insects. I saw the occasional leaping fish and then, very near the car park, I had a glimpse of an otter – just a brief break of the surface for air or in a manoeuvre on its prey. I could see the air bubbles heading downstream and so drifted with it and softly paddled. Two more fish leapt, but how that otter story ended would remain another mystery to entice me back.

With the river clearly getting busy and more accessible with lower water levels, I was now concerned that my cameras might draw attention to the beavers. So I wrote to my Wildlife Trust colleagues, inclined to break for a while.

The next week, the beavers appeared at the UK Annual Meeting of Triodos Bank. The event was hosted by the fantastic Gillian Burke of BBC *Springwatch* fame, and in my presentation, I unleashed my inner-*Springwatch* fan by showing a picture of a beaver and talking about the Eurasian beaver having successfully re-established itself in the landscape, using it as a metaphor for how banking needs to reintroduce values and consider sustainability, and how our different kind of bank was successfully establishing itself in the UK banking landscape. Of course, I gave no sense of where I had taken the picture, and when Gillian asked, I said I'd tell her later, only to never return to the subject. She did, however, ask if the picture had been taken between Bristol and Bath and implied she knew some people were taking reintroduction into their own hands and releasing beavers. I remember a *Springwatch* episode where Gillian went out on a paddleboard to explore a beaver pool at one of the reintroductions and hoped one day she might be able to tell the story of the Bristol beavers as a completely wild and free population. They are certainly free, and wherever they came from mattered less now than understanding their spread and avoiding any potential clashes with humans.

I am always drained for a few days after such big events as the annual meeting. I had put my all into preparing and delivering a speech, and once the adrenaline wore off, I had planned a quiet weekend to recover and wasn't planning to see the beavers. But come Saturday evening, I was a bit more energised, the weather was dull, and what else was I going to do? So I packed the kayak and had an early night before my ninth survey outing. Unfortunately, I was awake at 2am and restless until the alarm went off at 4am. Really? I am really going to do this? But I got going because the weather forecast – a little overcast but dry – looked promising for visibility on the river and for the wildlife staying up later in the morning.

As I drove over the hills approaching the valley, a fine but persistent drizzle hit the windscreen. I hoped it was just gathered on the hilltops, but though less persistent, it was still there when I arrived at the river. As I unloaded, to my amazement, a dog-walker appeared, and as I pushed off from the launch point at 5.30am, a group of runners was gathering. I have always tried to be very quiet setting up as there are houses on the opposite side of the road to the river and car park. The previous week I'd had the strange encounter with the guy staring at me and unresponsive when I waved good morning. He had then watched me launch and stared from the footbridge as I waved back even more obviously. I had paddled off feeling worried about the car being broken into or whether he was a local resident disgruntled by early visitors. But this comparatively bustling morning healed any worry or guilt that I was the only dawn-user of the car park.

The second I was on the water I felt better, head clearing, breathing deeper and energy lifting with the excitement of what may be ahead. As I made progress I saw a large single ripple ring in the centre of the river – otter, I thought. I paused and waited and then saw the splash of an otter's side or rear breaking the surface as it chased its prey. I was starting to read the signs of this river.

Today, however, I was focused on the survey, and in the drizzle, neither a potential otter shot nor even the teasing heron could tempt my camera out of the dry bag. Amy had emailed me survey sheets that she wanted me to start using, which replicated those used in the official beaver-reintroduction studies. They required a GPS location to record activity or sightings. So I downloaded an app to my phone that gave a GPS reading and took a screen shot of new activity at each location.

There was a lot to record: more bark-stripping and branch-cutting at the location I'd recorded over the past few weeks, and several smaller areas of activity, including on the aspen tree. The river was more swollen with recent rainfall but not fast flowing, and I was able to meander the banks. It is amazing how much the river landscape can change in a week. Reeds

that were only recently breaking the surface now towered a metre above it, concealing the view along parts of the river, and the lily pads fringing areas of the riverbank that, a week ago weren't even budding above the surface, now had yellow flowers bursting through.

I approached Beaver Alley as quietly as I could, soft paddle strokes gently moving me along. Hugging the right-hand bank closely, as I had done when I'd had my success getting a picture of a beaver, there was a sudden *splosh* just a few metres to my right under some overhanging willow.

I drifted, hoping for a glimpse of it, but all I could see were some signs of undercurrent where it must be swimming. Ten metres or so upriver, there was a *kerplunk* as an invisible beaver entered the water from an area of submerged and sprouting willow on the left bank – annoyingly, a feeding station where I had set a camera trap three times with no luck. Was this a second beaver?

I drifted again, paddle lying in my lap and camera at the ready in my hands. Nothing. A dipper flew up the river towards me and landed where the beaver had been. It gently dipped its way down the sloping bow and took a drink. I hadn't seen a dipper for years and got a few shots. Then, just as I moved on, there was a huge tail slap from within the same area of submerged willow. The beaver must have been watching me, just poking above the surface, and once my eyes were averted had thought it safe to alert any other beavers. I was now confident there had to be more than one beaver, as the culprit for the first splosh could not have crossed the river and climbed the branches on the opposite side without me seeing or hearing it exit the water.

I headed onward upriver, passing where the beavers lived and leaving them to return home for the day. I noted some new activity, and finding there was no activity near one camera trap, I left it where it was, as all my experimenting meant I knew the batteries should last another week if it hasn't been frequently triggered. I found a recently severed, five-metre willow branch, about 20 centimetres across, jammed up against the riverbank. It had several branches stemming from it and was clearly a project half-finished or a floating food store. Scouring the riverbank, I couldn't find where it had come from, but noticing past activity I realised that beavers can climb quite high and along quite thin branches. I also noticed that, though the riverbank theoretically had no private access, several points had been strimmed, presumably to enable river access for fishing.

I turned back to collect and swap camera traps and supped on some tea from my flask to warm up. As I drifted, I could hear a faint buzzing of an engine and assumed it was from somewhere along the railway. Then in the distance I saw the origin: a metal-bathtub of a fishing boat making its way upriver, powered by a noisy Seagull outboard motor. As we crossed, the two camouflaged fishermen aboard asked if I was fishing. "A different kind of fishing," I said, as I held up my camera. One shrugged apologetically, realising his noisy engine would have scared off any wildlife.

It was raining now as I collected the camera traps. I am a bit like a kid on Christmas Eve, wanting to have peak to see what might be inside before properly opening and finding out later. But the camera that had got me wet while placing it on a long pole wouldn't display, which I hoped was positive, perhaps because the batteries were low. I got a little less wet retrieving it and placed another long pole with a camera in a different location, angled to look from above onto the riverbank and water's edge.

Wet and cold, I paddled hard for home and only paused to take GPS readings where I had earlier seen the beavers splosh into the water and tail slap. But then I saw something intriguing floating in the middle of the river. It was pale, and from a distance I thought it would be discarded beaver bark, but as I drew alongside, I realised it was the underbelly of a mostly submerged, large, dead fish. It was a pike, which must have measured more than a metre as, beside the kayak, it went from my toes to lower thigh. It was exciting to find that such a magnificent predator roamed this river, though sad to see it as a corpse, with its eyes pecked out and algae clinging to its fins. I wondered why the body had surfaced now – perhaps internal gases made it buoyant or it had been stirred up from the deep by the boat motor – and what its fate had been, perhaps caught and released fatally injured by a sport fisherman. There was no obvious sign of external injury, and if I'd tried to lift it for closer inspection, its weight would have capsized me.

I got out of the river too fast, stumbled and soaked my right leg to my thigh, and being rain-drenched everywhere else, I got packed as quickly as I could. Once home, I went straight into a hot shower to warm up and then ate a second breakfast before unloading the kayak and collapsing in a chair. It was Father's Day, 20 June 2021, a day that always left me feeling a little numb and melancholic, having lost my father when I was 20, after several years of illness – pre-diagnosis of a terminal form of leukaemia and then a couple of years fighting on with blood transfusions and surgery. Grim. Not easy to deal with in your teens and something that stays with you. However, he told the parish priest in the days before he died that he had no regrets in life, which was some statement, given that he worked incredibly hard and was robbed of his retirement by illness. I do not want to regret having worked all hours and not having lived doing the other things that bring me joy and fulfilment. Something I should have remembered when debating whether to visit to the river that day.

Eventually I stirred from the chair, having had a brief nap along the way, and thought about downloading the cameras. There were more than 300 images and video clips on the one I had placed on the long pole. The cameras were now being triggered regularly by dragonflies and damselflies, but this time, most of the images were in night vision, and as I opened up the first series, I could clearly see a beaver with its back to the camera and its distinctive tail trailing down the riverbank. It must have emerged and climbed out there. Finally, a decent shot of a beaver.

I carried on scrolling to find more beaver images. Many were blurry as the beaver moved quickly or the camera fired too late and just caught the top of a head or leg, but I was delighted that all the experimentation and straining to get a camera in the right spot had finally paid off. There was also one amusing 'before, during and after' series (see opposite), where the willow vegetation that partly concealed the camera was set upon by the beaver, removing it to provide a clear view of the riverbank. This beaver had ambitions of fame!

I then found I had a lot to thank that beaver for. As I continued scrolling, I suddenly sat back as a much larger beaver popped onto my screen, huge in fact. This was an altogether different muscly animal with a much larger and wider tail. My mind was racing. This was definitive proof that there was more than one. I flipped back to the first image to compare the proportions of the two animals against the vegetation. Could it be? The first picture was obviously a kit and the second an adult beaver. Wow! How I could I have

missed that? I realised all of the short films were of the kit, and I now had a wealth of behavioural footage, from feeding to scratching and grooming and even one with it using its tucked tail as a seat, which they are renowned for doing. I then found I had a photo of the adult and kit together. And when I played the film taken after the photo series, I saw there were two kits! The adult was dragging a branch out of the water, with the kit closely inspecting and exploring it, when a second kit emerged from the river to join them. I hadn't just established there was more than one but proved there was an entire family with at least two kits.

I was so excited and emotional, partly because of all the effort it had taken to get to this point but also because I was so inspired by the beavers that I had a lump in my throat as I stared deeply into pictures and watched and repeated the short films. It was mesmerising.

I had to tell someone and called my former Chair of Trustees at the Wildlife Trust, Roz Kidman Cox, as she'd known what I was trying to do and would understand what it meant to me and the significance of the news. Roz is someone who has a deep passion for wildlife and is absorbed in it through her work as former editor of *BBC Wildlife* magazine, now book editor and chair of judges for Wildlife Photographer of the Year among many other things. She immediately understood the excitement and significance, and I was so grateful to share that moment because life is

somewhat lonely and empty if it isn't shared, and for one reason or another, life for me is less shared nowadays, something I hoped might change with a little restoration of myself and my energy. Some of my biggest successes in my career have been the emptiest moments of my life because they haven't been shared deeply with someone else. This moment had a great sense of achievement partly for the physical and technical challenges but also because I'd managed to find beavers, see them, photograph them, work out where they lived and then, by trial and error, managed to film and photograph them with some intimacy. These were never going to be award-winning images, but they were perfect.

As I studied more and more of the mini-clips and pictures, I was intrigued by how dextrous the kit's front paws were, almost human in their

movement and grip. When tagging turtles on Australia's Barrow Island, I remember seeing a turtle skeleton and being struck by how each limb ended in five digits, resembling human hands and feet. You would never appreciate that when looking at the four flippers of a live turtle, or that their digits are dextrous, as I witnessed when watching them digging out their egg-laying chambers. The contrast between the beavers' little 'hands' and their powerful webbed hind paws is incredible.

I also noticed the speed at which the beavers devour food. The kits were consuming willow shoots their own body length in a few seconds, and the adult beaver would chomp through a five-centimetre-thick branch in just a few bites, the fleshy wood crumbling under the power of its jaws. I also noticed that beavers don't share food. One clip showed an adult buffeting a

kit away from its main-course branch, and another a kit comically running away from its sibling into the river clasping a thin willow shoot, despite being surrounded by a bounty of shoots.

The footage also proved some of my earlier theories right. Not just the location of the burrow and the regular use of the area of muddy bank but also that there was a food cache next to the entrance. I had noticed its mass had been declining, but I now realised that the female beaver would have probably been consuming it until the emergence of her kits. The footage also appeared to show a beaver pulling up a branch from underneath all of the submerged willow, so the food cache probably included an underwater larder of softened woody treats. I would later learn they stockpile underwater to provide a safe and accessible food store if the water freezes.

The clips also showed why the beavers had stayed closer to home in recent weeks – the emergence of the kits.

Except for a brief nap, I had been awake since 2am, yet the writing had been flowing, and before long another 3,000 words had been written – and I still had energy for more. Something new was emerging in my own rewilding and reconnection. Before bed that evening, I shared some of the best pictures and clips with Wildlife Trust colleagues, who replied almost instantly with equal excitement and disbelief. Days later, when I was just relaxing with a cuppa and watching some of the clips again, I realised the footage was taken over several days, but the really special clip of the adult with the kits was taken on 17 June, the date of the annual meeting where I had shown the beaver photo and used the re-establishment of beavers as a metaphor for what banking should be doing.

I had got so excited by the pictures and footage that I almost forgot about the second camera. There weren't any beaver clips, just the usual pigeon baths, etc., though a beautiful wren perched on a willow branch was another to add to the list of many birds using the chaotic structures that the felled and submerged willow limbs create. There was, however, an intriguing photo: a picture of a mink, no less. I then looked back at a blurry picture from the other camera that, in my excitement, I'd just skipped past, and sure enough, another fast-moving American mink. It was what I had mistaken for the end of a domestic cat's tail on an earlier haul of images, and it was clearly visiting the area regularly, using the pathways created by the beavers. One shot showed a mink jumping into the vegetation to the side of the beaver track, and then another very blurred image showed it pouncing on a poor unsuspecting pigeon, which was just walking down to its local for a drink.

Otter, mink, pike. This was a river full of predators, and given otter and mink reportedly predate very young beaver kits, it makes beaver establishment here even more remarkable. I wondered now about trying to get a better image of the mink as a side project, surmising I'd need a faster camera. But first I needed to understand what would be useful for the Trust and its fundraising ambitions to create a project to support the beavers' prosperity and, as a result, nature's wider restoration.

I had planned to meet with Amy by the river one evening the following weekend, but she wasn't well and had to cancel, and I ended up taking a week off visiting the river. I had two cameras in place and wanted to give the one I had speculatively placed on a potential feeding station time to catch a beaver. However, I was also at something of a crossroads, as I now had enough evidence of the beavers – where they lived and that they were a breeding family. So what was my purpose now?

6 Reflections on the river

I had been back at work almost a month, and on three weekends had still gone out at dawn to visit the beavers. Now it was catching up with me. The return to work had been intense, and with a number of big things to prepare for and deliver, I was feeling tired and decided to take a weekend off from beaver patrol. The beavers still gave me great delight and energy, but I was also doing little else in my spare time between preparing kit and cameras, loading and unloading the kayak and the five-hour round trips to survey the river, and then downloading the photographs and sharing and writing up a report. I could see why the Trust needed extra resources, as it would be a lot of work to survey areas properly and monitor any migration, with the real task being to engage landowners and stakeholders so the spread of beavers could be supported and bring the benefits of restoring the natural landscape.

The Trust was about to submit another attempt at a funding bid. Now that there was proof of a breeding family, surely funding would be forthcoming, both to monitor their spread and their impact on biodiversity. I mischievously thought to suggest a bid to local government for monitoring the spread of pest and vermin and harm to humans – depressingly likely to be more successful. Julie asked me to write some text to include in the bid to give personal perspective on what I had experienced, which I gladly did. Doing so made me reflect on how remarkable it was that beavers were thriving on this river. Large lengths of the riverbanks are eroded where grazing sheep and cattle come down to drink, a kilometre of riverbank has been lost to a metal-and-brick railway embankment, and the connection to the wider landscape has been lost through its dissection by human infrastructure, not to mention all the swimmers, fishermen and motor boats. If beavers (and otters) can survive and thrive here, then we have hope – hope of being able to restore biodiversity and live in greater harmony alongside it.

My writing still had no purpose other than as a means to keep my adventures alive, connect with what was going on for me and identify what I was feeling and wanting to do. I had let the '15 minutes of writing a day' slip but was finding time a couple of evenings a week and at weekends, which was making me reflect. I was also seeing the shoots of a story emerge, with links to aspects of my life and career.

My photographic skill and equipment remained very amateur, though I have a decent camera and telephoto lens. The challenge of trying to capture the beavers had definitely triggered me to want to take better pictures, and my mind was often filled with notions of placing a camera underwater or ways of getting a better-quality motion-sensor camera placed on the burrow for those beautiful kits. I even plunged into internet research.

I'd also have moments of reality check, questioning how much it would cost and why bother, given you can easily get clearer pictures on one of the beaver-release areas, where the beavers are more accepting of human presence. A friend had just visited Otterton in Devon, and the female beaver there was very active despite the obvious human presence on the bridge and gathered viewers on the riverbank, giving all great views and photographs. While I was still keen to get pictures, was that really what was motivating me?

Having the weekend off from my own beaver patrol meant I'd decided to go for a cycle ride. But when I went to the garage on Sunday morning just before 8am, I discovered it had been burgled overnight. The irony is that, had I been up at 4am as usual for my survey, I might have caught the culprits, as the break-in took place between 1.30am, when my neighbours retired, and 6.30am, when I had got up. Cycle and car accessories as well as tools were stolen in the haul, which was themed around metal that no doubt could be easily sold as scrap. Thankfully none of the kayak's metal paddles or wheels were taken, though I did have to explain to the police why the stolen goods included a WWI bayonet knife and WWII Gurkha kukri knife. These were heirlooms gifted to me as a teenager when enthralled with family war heroes. But if you choose to believe that everything in life happens for a positive reason, their disappearance now was perhaps symbolic of something shifting. Whilst my uncle who fought in WWII will always be a hero to me, I'd kept them for decades out of duty, no longer enamoured with war and conflict.

I have been burgled several times in my life, and while it used to feel a huge personal invasion, I am quite hardened to it now. While I'd love to give the culprits a piece of my mind, I also see the real problem being poverty and other social issues. We can never truly achieve a sustainable society unless we address social and environmental issues holistically, as I found when spending months volunteering as a conservation diver in a remote part of the Philippines, where dynamite fishing had been practised. People striving for basic subsistence sought the easiest way to catch the most fish, blowing them up by dropping a lit dynamite stick into the water and then picking up the fish off the surface. It gave a rich bounty but also destroyed the very reefs that sustained the fish.

This was an extreme example, but without social-welfare systems and greater equality in the distribution of wealth, people will always exploit the environment to survive or get on in life.

I had dinner with some friends later that week, and while keeping the river and location a secret, I told them what I'd been up to, and it was great to be able to share it. My friend Dominic Hogg was even more excited by the otter encounters and the picture I'd managed to take, and I promised to take him upriver someday. It was also good to be able to talk to people who understood where I was at in life and who recognised the need for change. I'd become stuck, which had been exacerbated by the Covid-19 lockdowns, and while I completely have perspective on them being first-world problems, I was single, had lived in the same flat for 10 years and become too old and grumpy to have occasionally noisy neighbours above me, while also craving to have nature 'right there' rather than a journey away. I was also reflecting a lot after five years as CEO of Triodos Bank, and in my ninth year as a CEO in total, what I wanted to do next, both with the bank and beyond. I wasn't in flow. The day after that dinner, Dom's wife Rita, who is a spiritualist and healer, texted me:

> *"I was thinking about how you have attracted beavers into your life. They're masters of blocking things up and causing dramatic shifts in direction. That's so interesting because you've been feeling quite blocked and could really do with a change in direction. I think they're mirroring you in some way and have gone to some trouble to find you to help move you forward. I reckon they're your totemic spiritual power animal! Thank them and ask them to show you the way."*

If they had been trying to find me, then the illusive buggers had a funny way of showing it! However, the sentiment that this purpose and my connection to the beavers had arrived at a key point in my life was one I very much shared, and it made me realise that more time on the river and with the beavers might bring the reflection and shift in flow that I needed. I packed the kayak and kit that evening to set off at dawn the following morning.

Before going to bed, I viewed the forecast, which was for rain overnight but clearing about 5am, with a chance of showers thereafter. I was fast asleep when the alarm went off at 4am. I looked out, and the persistent rain from the storm had already passed. Ten minutes into the journey, heavy rain hit the car, but when I launched the kayak, there was just a very light drizzle.

I paddled my route, giving my morning salute to the heron as it took off from its hidden perch, no doubt cursing the interruption of its breakfast. In revenge, I think it summoned a heavy downpour that started to boil the river's surface, and I had to paddle fast to shelter under the road bridge.

I got caught in rain again at the furthest point of the trip, and as I worked my way downstream, I hugged the riverbank to get as much shelter as I could from overhanging trees – a kingfisher taking flight each time I got too close. Not wanting to disturb an entourage of some 30 Canada geese drifting towards me and stretching impressively across the breadth of the river, I finally turned back. As I skirted the river's edge, I saw that the beaver-coppiced willow trees were full of the tents of small ermine moth caterpillars in huge abundance. I could see the web of cotton-like tents higher up in the willows, but by far the greater density was in the lower branches coppiced closer to the riverbank, which must have been more sheltered. The pale yellow caterpillars hung in their wispy hammocks – yet another beneficiary

of the beavers' tree surgery and habitat creation, which in turn provides food for bats, birds and many others in the food chain.

Before I reached the farthest point in my paddle, I approached Beaver Alley slowly with gentle paddle strokes. As it was now not raining, I got the camera out of the dry bag and hugged the right-hand riverbank, looking through my binoculars on every few strokes. Nothing. A few strokes more, nothing. On I went. Then as I paused in my stroke and reached for my binoculars, a huge splosh to my left on the opposite bank. I had no chance of seeing it advance as it was on the far side of some dense willow stalks that had previously been beaver-coppiced, and it must have seen me only as I drew level with it and into view around the corner of the willow.

My heart still jumps into my mouth when they splosh or tail slap unexpectedly in dramatic contrast to the silence and calm of early morning. I waited, drifting on the river, but saw no sign of air bubbles or a head popping up to swim. It was about 20 metres to the burrow, and I presumed it swam straight back under the cover of the limbs, protecting the location of what I believed to be the main underwater entrance. I had come to realise how lucky I had been to take just a few photographs of the swimming beaver on just my third trip on the water. I was now in double figures for beaver patrols, and while I had seen beavers clearly on four occasions, I had only had that one opportunity to take a picture. Having got close to beavers inadvertently so many times, I now suspected that, like those other large, furry mammals badgers, beavers must have fairly poor eyesight and that, perhaps, their swimmers' ears also prevent them from detecting me earlier.

This time, I'd noticed lots of new bark-stripping activity, particularly in the farthest stretch of the river, so perhaps the mother was eating to replenish her reserves after months of birthing and nursing, or maybe the whole family is venturing farther now the kits have emerged. I took pictures on my phone and GPS readings and while doing so noticed the area where I had speculatively left a camera had been thoroughly mown, suggesting it might become a feeding station. Fantastic! If I'd placed the camera with the angle I'd envisaged, I should have a clear view of a beaver eating the willow shoots all along the length of the twisted fallen limb. Excited to get home and view the pictures, I collected that camera and another by the burrow and left two in different locations where I'd had success previously.

I had just finished putting the cameras out and pushed off when two paddleboarders appeared downriver in the distance. I drifted gently along as they came powering up and exchanged a pleasantry, bemoaning the warm but tropical showery conditions. After a little while I turned and paddled back upriver to watch from a distance as they passed the burrow, oblivious to my cameras and the burrow's existence. I headed back and got a shock as I rounded some reeds in a bend in the river. A fisherman was tucked into the riverbank under his shelter. I paddled around his line, and in soft voices, we exchanged equal surprise as he waved me on my passage.

Returning home, after a replenishing plate of toast and tea, I felt chuffed on finding that the camera trap I had speculatively placed on the opposite bank and 20 metres upriver to the burrow had been triggered more than 250 times over the nearly four weeks I had left it, hoping for activity on what I thought were willow shoots ripe for beaver dining.

Wading through the images, I could see I had hundreds of pictures of Canada geese using the limb as a safe haven for their fast-growing and now half-adult-sized goslings, but there was also some night footage. Sure enough, there were some good shots and films of a beaver grazing the limb bald. One film even showed the beaver clambering along its length and making a very unstylish river-entry splash. However, the really interesting thing was that, though I had at first thought this individual was an adult, its tail was far too small, yet it was also bigger than the kits, who could not have grown that much in just two weeks. When I looked in detail at the footage of the kits, you could see that their tails weren't much longer than their hind legs. The beaver on the feeding station had a tail more than half its body length, which meant it had to be a yearling.

So there were at least five individuals, which meant beavers had been breeding there for two years or more. The relative size was confirmed by another image of my nemesis, the heron, perched on the same branch, showing the yearling was about half the size of the heron, so neither adult nor kit. Kits are 300-700 grams when born and take at least two years to be sexually mature, and a full-grown adult can weigh up to 35 kilograms

and can be as long as 1.35 metres. The yearling was a significant discovery, confirming that this was a multi-generational, well established family. I was also pleased with the pictures and film. The beaver was beautifully framed in the centre of the branch, the background trees softly lit by the travelling infrared light, contrasting with the dark river surface.

When I then checked the footage on the camera I had left at the burrow, at a different angle to the last placing, it had been triggered more than 400 times, mostly by the two young kits together, still small and clumsy. While I had to weed out dozens of half-shots or blurred images where they had moved too fast, I had more than 30 decent pictures or clips of the kits grooming, swimming, eating, following mum and greeting one another in moments of intimacy, as well as quality footage of the impressively large and powerful female. The pictures showed that the kits were staying close to the burrow and dipping in and out of the water, protected by the maze of willow, and that mum occasionally visited, leaving small branches and shoots on the bank for the kits. However, the kits were clearly learning fast, and as they explored their new world, they had grazed most of the shoots and young branches that provided cover. I had also got the first dawn/dusk daylight images and could now see the beavers' magnificent reddish-brown fur – most vivid when dry.

My 'totem animal' had led me to a new discovery and shown me unexpected new beauty and intimacy, and my reflection now was to continue to follow them and see what else I might learn. Another reflection was just to play and let purpose subside in importance. I'd continue to collect data and images for the Trust, but from now on, I'd also be as playful with camera placement as I had been with the speculative location, and just see what happened.

My random writing was flowing as it often did after time on the river, and I also noticed I needed time away from it to walk and think in order to make sense of what I wanted to capture and convey. I would often message myself from my phone with a line on something I wanted to write about or research, and the intensity of my thoughts was deepening to levels reminiscent of writing up my PhD some 21 years before and rarely experienced since. These beavers were showing me the way back.

7 Birthday gifts

It was my birthday, and I had been tracking the beavers for just over two months. I love to immerse myself in the natural world early on the morning of my birthday and on Christmas Day. Some of my best memories are of those mornings, including a cold, sunny Christmas morning watching three kingfishers fishing close together, and a slightly more tropical Christmas, scuba diving in Indonesia and finding the boat in the middle of a super-pod of hunting dolphins.

On this morning, I rose early as usual so I could be on the river before the sun was up, but I was tired after the adrenaline of hosting a visit of HRH The Princess Royal the day before. The visit had been arranged by HM Lord Lieutenant Peaches Golding OBE, to mark 25 years of Triodos Bank advocating for a more sustainable finance system in the UK (and 40 years internationally). It was one of the more surreal days in my life as a CEO, but Princess Anne was impressively knowledgeable and genuinely engaged on a wide range of environmental issues as well as important social issues such as digital inclusion. Nature restoration was clearly a passion, and we touched on work Triodos is leading to create new models for investing in nature, for example, by contracting water companies, insurers and flood agencies to make payments for the restoration of a canalised river and to enable flooding of drained land.

Our royal visit wasn't the only news of the week. The National Trust had done some very clever PR by announcing the first beavers to be born on Exmoor in 400 years, with one being named after the Manchester United and England footballer Marcus Rashford in recognition of his brilliant campaigning on food poverty – a feel-good story that ran nationally. However, this was a family specifically reintroduced and photographed at that location. The Bristol Avon beavers were an unreported and seemingly undiscovered population of several generations. So I wondered what future headlines they might grab in comparison. Perhaps when they are unveiled we will learn whether someone had a role in their being on the Avon in the first place.

As I travelled to the river, the sky was filled with soft pastel colours, peach rising to yellow and then powder blue. It really was a beautiful clear-sky morning at the start of what was forecast to be a roasting hot day. When I went to put the kayak onto the water, a large willow tree was lying in the water across the launch area. There was still just room to push the kayak between the lying limbs and the riverbank, and I paddled around the drooping branches to inspect. The willow appeared to have fallen naturally, the lower water levels and drying mud banks causing the weight of the tree to pull it over into the river. There was no sign of the beavers having had any role in its collapse, though there were signs they had discovered it, with several small branches distinctively cut off to a pencil point and some coppicing of stems mid-river. It was a clear indication that the beavers were roaming their territory farther again, perhaps now the kits had acclimatised to the outside world. It did, however, raise the concern that their activity might be noticed, as this launch point would inevitably be heavily used in the fine weather. Several trees had clearly been cut back by saws where they had caused an obstruction, and hopefully this one would be trimmed back soon and avoid the potential for beavers being blamed for its demise.

I paddled through a light haze rather than the dense fog of previous trips and was greeted by a kingfisher flying straight towards me mid-river, exposing its bronzed underside as it turned into the riverbank. Two kingfishers then teased me as I continued upriver by never giving me a

chance of a photograph. Trying not to get too distracted by the regular flashes of blue lightning, I found the beavers had also revisited two feeding stations they had not visited for some considerable time.

Close by, a buzzard started calling, to be followed by a slightly haunting squawk from further up the riverbank, and then another, lighter cry from the opposite riverbank. The three buzzards continued calling, and as the sun hit the tops of the trees, I could see the first adult almost above me. I stayed still, trying to take some photographs of this majestic raptor, who gave me a full view before moving behind me. The second adult then revealed itself with a call before flying to join its partner. The lighter call continued, and I paddled on softly, passing the tree harbouring what I assumed to be a young buzzard calling to its parents. It was a magical moment to savour as I stealthily moved on upriver and into Beaver Alley.

The calm river meant I could move much more quietly than ever before and could scan ahead through binoculars, camera ready in my lap.

I couldn't see any movement but just sensed I was being watched. I paused, paddled softly, then paused again. The silence was broken by a huge tail-slap immediately to my left, which set my heart pounding with the shock. A large, powerful beaver had made that noise and the subsequent waves. Same area, similar time (6.05am) to all my other sightings. One day I might be lucky enough to spot one first, though the now-abundant cover from the sprouting coppiced willows meant it was a lot less likely than when I first managed to photograph a beaver mid-river.

In water, the particles are much closer together than in air, and that density means vibration energy can quickly transmit from one particle to the next, and a sound wave travels more than four times faster than it would in air. So a tail-slap is a far more effective means of warning than a verbal one. However, it takes a lot of energy to create the sound wave.

Continuing upriver past the burrow, I discovered the large mid-river willow tree that defined Beaver Alley was now at 45 degrees and blocking two thirds of the channel. The beavers had stripped bark on its largest limbs both above and below the waterline. I navigated around the new blockade to inspect the partly exposed root ball and again couldn't see any signs that the tree's collapse was caused by the beavers. So perhaps the lower water level meant the drying mud bank had again just given way. However, the large areas of golden-white exposed flesh meant it was now very obvious to anyone who knew the signs that beavers were present, and they could easily be blamed for the blockage of a large section of the channel to small motor boats. Canoes, kayaks and paddleboards could still pass on either side of the tree, but if a boat tried the right-hand side, it would snag its propellers on the submerged trunk. I don't believe beavers were responsible, unless their weight when climbing forced the tipping point, but their opportunistic feeding meant the risk of their discovery loomed large. On the positive side, they were clearly enjoying the new beaver buffet.

The sun was now rising, lifting the haze from the river. Suddenly, on the right riverbank, on the bare branches at the top of an ash tree suffering from ash dieback, I spotted two cormorants lit up by the sun. They were some 15 miles inland, but the clear, calm river must have provided great fishing – once the annoying kayaker got out of their way. I have utmost respect for cormorants, having once had a dive in Mexico interrupted by them. They were diving down into schools of sardines. Following them into the clouds of small fish, trying to photograph them on the hunt, I witnessed how hard they have to work for a meal and how well adapted and agile they are below water. The petroleum-like sheen on their feathers created an underwater image I will never forget.

Further upriver I found more new beaver willow coppicing, and I took a GPS reading to add to the survey data. In the clear water I could see the extensive root systems that had sprouted from the submerged network of branches, the result of the beavers' tree surgery and engineering. A pair of mute swans were feeding on the roots at one of the feeding stations, giving another demonstration of the beavers' value to other species.

The previous silence was now steadily being broken by traffic noise echoing through the valley, and I could hear trains on the line. Turning back, I drifted on the flow, sipping a ginger tea poured from my flask and typing some survey notes into my phone. Passing slowly by, I noticed several limbs of previously submerged willow had been stripped of their bark, reinforcing the evidence that beavers have been present for some time.

I arrived back at the burrow area to rotate and set the cameras, remembering on this occasion to set the date – my birthday! The kits had now stripped large areas of the vegetation that had provided cover, and

I hypothesised that I must have caught them on camera shortly after they first emerged, because it was only in the past few weeks that the feeding activity had been concentrated around the burrow. Eurasian beavers mate from December to February, with a gestation period of approximately 100 days, and the kits remain in the lodge or burrow for one or two months, feeding on their mother's milk and small twigs and leaves brought in for them. If the timing of my first pictures correlated with their likely first emergence, it explained why the cameras were so unsuccessful previously.

I headed for home, despairing at the glut of Himalayan balsam now in flower on parts of the riverbank. It has large, pink flowers shaped like a bonnet and was introduced as a garden plant in 1839 before anyone really thought of concepts such as biosecurity or invasive species. It soon escaped gardens and became widely naturalised along riverbanks and ditches, as well as along roads and railway lines. It is fast-growing and spreads quickly, invading wet habitat and outcompeting native plants. Its explosive seedpods send its seeds into the river, dispersing them downstream. It flowers from July to October and is a constant pain for conservationists, who try to pull it up before flowering.

What a pity beavers don't eat Himalayan balsam, I thought. I ignored the teasing kingfishers, upped a heron from a perch where I'd previously seen a human fisherman and ducked under the fallen willow tree by the car park, extracting myself and the kayak, ready to roam again another day. I had felt strong on the river today. The calm water helped, as did the July warmth, and my paddle strokes felt effortless, despite a tiring few days and a short sleep. I sensed the connection of the psychological to the physical as I felt relaxed and looked forward to a day off, hoping my feeling of energy returning was something of a corner turned.

The buzzards and cormorants had been special moments, but I obviously hoped a proper beaver sighting might be my birthday present from nature. It wasn't until I started reviewing the contents of the camera traps that

I found my real present. One camera had only been triggered by a large rat and canoes and paddleboards that had clipped the corner of the sensors' range. However, the other camera had more than 900 images and film clips – a revelation of how much capacity the memory card had, let alone the durability of the rechargeable batteries. Over the next few days, I'd spend hours wading through it all, while trying to shake off the side-effects of my second Covid vaccination.

The clips showed that the kits were constantly at the entry/exit point, kept relatively hidden by the network of submerged branches, only briefly going into the water and, I assumed, back into the burrow via its underwater entrance. It was literally a beaver nursery, with adults regularly visiting the kits, leaving small branches or cuttings near the riverbank crèche. In contrast to the yearling I had captured upriver, the kits were awkward and clumsy. My present came in the discovery that there were in fact three kits, all caught briefly together in one clip. There was also a clip of the yearling

(who I'd never captured on camera at the nursery) being pushed away and off into the river by an adult. Adults can chase away their mature offspring, though if there are no suitable habitats for them to migrate to, beaver families are also known to stay with non-breeding adults. It could have been the yearling's time to leave home, or maybe the parents were simply keeping the nursery area and readily available food just for the kits.

The photographs and footage also showed two adults grooming one another, several intimate moments between an adult and a kit, an adult feeding on a willow branch in broad technicolour daylight – and a kit eating Himalayan balsam! Whether the latter is regularly eaten or if the youngster was just trying out the full available menu, I have no idea.

One clip showed two kits having a grumpy moment over a willow shoot, which confirmed my previous observation that beavers don't like to share food – and given the abundance of fast-sprouting willow and other vegetation, why should they? Amid the impressive haul of images, one of the prolific-oak-planting jay was added to the list of birds using the beaver-created bathing and drinking amenities.

The confirmation of three kits and at least one yearling was significant because it pointed to the likelihood that the beavers would spread. The Bristol Avon offers a wealth of possibilities. The river rises not that far away, just north of the village of Acton Turville in South Gloucestershire, and it flows through Wiltshire, then Bath and Bristol and out to the Severn Estuary. It is the UK's nineteenth-longest river and gives the beavers access to 121 kilometres (75 miles) of river to spread along. The total catchment area is some 2,220 square kilometres (860 square miles), presenting many further opportunities along its tributaries, with access to the nearby By Brook and the River Frome. Essentially, there was now a very real possibility that this thriving population would spread throughout the catchment. That possibility in itself was a birthday gift.

What it highlighted, however, was that, as the beavers spread, so would the risk of them coming into contact and possible conflict with humans. AWT was still awaiting the outcome of more funding bids that would enable it to not only monitor the population but also engage with landowners to make sure the beavers could spread without any conflict.

8 Our own extinction

In the UK, beavers were hunted to extinction for their fur, for food – the tail considered a delicacy at one time – for medicinal benefits thought to derive from the castoreum produced by their scent glands, and because they were seen as pests affecting tree crops and causing flooding to farmland. The beavers also suffered as a result of many myths, including being accused of eating fish and thus competing with people, and at one time, even being classified as fish.

Given past persecution, it is now our responsibility to support the emerging populations and enable them to connect and spread. This will also be to our own benefit. I have witnessed the role their tree surgery and engineering plays in slowing water, removing silt and building soil, as well as benefiting a wide variety of other wildlife including fish. Not to promote beavers in our landscape would be shortsighted. We can no longer see the world in a binary way with no balance between an extremely extractive economy and the natural world from which our wealth has been derived and upon which our future prosperity, health and even survival depends. We can't expect to maintain the status quo without consequences.

At the time of writing, in summer 2021, record heat waves in North America and record floods in large parts of Western Europe have shocked climate scientists as extremes beyond what their models had predicted. Extreme flooding is also happening in India and in China, where the extent of rainfall delivered a reality check on our resilience to the extremes of climate change. In the UK we have seen the highest temperature on record (in Northern Ireland) and many other temperature or rainfall records for a single day broken. The climate emergency is here, but despite many governments, parliaments and businesses declaring there is one, few are reacting as if it is an emergency.

In August 2021, the Intergovernmental Panel on Climate Change (IPCC) published a report stating the climate situation was now partly irreversible and represented a 'code red' for humanity. This was in a week amid record wildfires in parts of North America and Europe and when the first half of 2021 was confirmed as the period with the highest average land and sea temperatures on record. But no government ministers stood at a lectern delivering their emergency responses and plans. The climate and biodiversity crises have yet to prompt the same political responses as the pandemic did, despite the forecast collapse of ecosystems being by far the greatest emergency threatening humanity.

In the same recent weeks, we have had billionaires Richard Branson and Jeff Bezos both take the first tourist flights to space, with another billionaire Elon Musk also in the race to create the first successful space-tourism business. Will history look kindly on these huge egos racing to a hedonistic goal of spending 10 minutes in space and burning extraordinary amounts of fossil fuel in the process? I doubt it. History will probably astound at why men with such power didn't race to save the Amazon (the rainforest, not Jeff Bezos's company) or indeed the Virgin Islands from rising sea levels and ocean acidification. Rather than compete, couldn't they all work together on one goal?

Change takes bravery, and change needs vision. The climate emergency will not be solved by new energy sources, better-insulated homes and electric cars alone. Fundamentally we need to evolve better connections with one another and be prepared to share resources to ensure everyone has their needs met, focus less on material wealth and more on wellbeing, and work as communities rather than competing individuals. The concept of sustainability needs to have social and cultural considerations at its core, as wonderfully articulated in Kate Raworth's book on her theory of 'doughnut economics', where society and the economy is run to ensure everyone lives above a minimum level of subsistence but that collectively we don't live beyond our planetary boundaries. Essentially, we need to live within our means for the benefit of all and in consideration of future generations.

While such thinking is permeating mainstream debate more and more, few are advocating real change. Those that are tend to be long-term campaigners who have just found a new way to communicate the issues. One exception is Mary Portas – the embodiment of capitalist consumerism, powering high-street brands to sales success and excess, convincing shoppers that their growing wealth must be spent on the latest must-have fashion and fuelling our throw-away single-use society. Not anymore. Open about her role in fuelling the fires, Mary has become a great advocate for how wrong our economic model is and its disconnection from environmental and social outcomes. "Objects don't change who you are or how you feel about yourself," she says in her book *Rebuild* – an accessible and clear articulation of how we need to change our view of business and, indeed, how we all need to evolve in parallel to that. In the book, she mentions Triodos Bank, based on an interview I did for her 'Kindness Economy' podcast and quotes my thoughts about the most successful businesses of the future being those that can demonstrate the highest levels of social and environmental consciousness. I believe we are at the start of a great awakening, in which increasing environmental disasters will bring demands for social change, and fast. The question is whether that change will be too little too late.

For the type of change and action we need, John Elkington's *Green Swans* and Jonathon Porrit's *Hope in Hell* are deeper works from two great thinkers whom I have admired for years. I cannot bring their polymath knowledge and vision to the problems, but I do know that the current lip service we see paid to the issues is only going to make things worse. Yes, we have a UK government with a ten-point plan, but this is just a well-meaning start and seeks to convince us that a few changes here and there will make everything alright. There is no vision or honesty on how much our lives will need to change and how we will have to adapt, and there is no sense of the climate 'emergency' parliament has declared. The pandemic has shown us what an emergency reaction looks like and how the government machine can move when the leadership demands that it does.

In the 50 or so years from John F Kennedy's presidency of the US to Barrack Obama's presidency, the population of the world doubled. It continues to grow at pace and could reach nine billion people by 2050. A few more wind farms and more tree-planting isn't going to be nearly enough of a shift that we have to make as individuals, as communities and as a global inclusive society. The issues facing us are not just more extreme-weather events and further pandemics but potentially the collapse of societies.

Extinction Rebellion (XR), together with the inspiring Fridays For Future school-strike climate movement, have done more to prompt action than any other environmental movements I have seen since the mid-1990s. Indeed, we wouldn't have net-zero carbon targets enshrined in legislation without the XR movement. However, few give them credit, and most of the media chose to report XR's past protests with a negative tone. That no doubt reflects widespread public opinion on the challenges the disruptions create, but surely the media also has a responsibility to give much deeper attention to the issues at stake and scrutinise government action, or inaction, as well. In April 2019, at the height of XR's protests, the media tone was turning against the protests and focusing on the costs of business closures or lost customers.

This indeed is a serious issue for those affected but pales into insignificance compared to the costs to business and the instability we face if we do not start to treat climate change as an emergency. I was part of a group of business leaders who wrote an open letter in *The Times* on Easter Monday 2019 advocating this argument. That we were covered on BBC Radio 4's *Today* programme was a small victory in bringing a longer-term view back into the debate.

Media bias and dumbing-down are issues that need to change. For years the BBC had a policy of giving equal voice to completely unfounded and unevidenced opinions on the myths of climate change because it wanted to give both sides of the argument. This stance being mirrored in other institutions has set back efforts to tackle climate change by years if not decades. We now need to debate on how public-service broadcasting should be rekindled. The BBC already spends significant effort having to justify itself, which will increase with pressures to reduce its dependency on the licence fee and in turn make the entire media system open to the manipulation and bias of those that own the commercial outlets.

Throughout my career, I've questioned the integrity of the wider media, based on experiences. These include being partially and misleadingly quoted by *The Times* in an article on Brexit, a senior editor of *The Guardian* suggesting they would do a feature on the bank provided we were prepared to take a political stance on an issue and, most recently, *The Daily Telegraph* running a completely incorrect and misleading article. I read and hear all news now with watchful and distrustful eyes and ears. Wouldn't it be great if some of the billionaires mentioned earlier acquired media outlets to show us the Earth and our relationship with it as it really needs to be seen rather than superficially from space. We desperately need a less shallow media that is not led so much by public opinion and what sells.

The lessons from various threads of my career, from household-waste recycling to the debacle of Portbury Wharf, is that we need to communicate and to lead through change. My experience in leadership is that, if you think you are communicating enough, do more. It is the single most important element of change management, and we need government, the media, businesses and high-profile figures to do much more in taking responsibility for our climate and ecological emergencies. My rant about the media reflects my long-term interest in systemic change. During the early part of my career, when trying to stimulate investment in a growing UK recycling industry, I met with the barrier of vested interest and greed from one of the UK's largest banks. "At the end of the day the return on investment on a landfill site is better the faster you fill it," I was told. This was a defining moment, when I became dissatisfied working just at a grassroots level and became interested in systems change and the levers of power.

Grassroots action and activism remain vital, which is one reason I still happily volunteer physically and support various organisations in other ways where I can. But the scale of systems change we need is immense. Our financial, food, transport and energy systems – and even our political system – need overhauling if we are to make the transition to live within the realms of 'doughnut economics'.

I also foresee the way we organise conservation having to change. If we are to move to an economy where nature is inherently valued and placed at its centre, then financial institutions, businesses and governments will have to fund nature's restoration in a different way. At present most are still confusing 'net zero' carbon targets with being 'carbon neutral'. The latter means offsetting your impacts, which is ultimately flawed, as there simply isn't enough land on the planet to plant all the trees we would need, nor the peat bogs to restore, and so on. Net zero means each country, business and financial institution having a net-zero impact, i.e., if you are a bank, the carbon emissions from your lending and investment portfolio of property, manufacturing and everything else are 'net' in balance with the carbon absorbed by your portfolio, such as from financing sustainable forestry, regenerative agriculture and nature-based solutions for flood management. Net-zero targets do not just mean a shift in how we do things, they require

the creation of a whole new concept of economy that finances nature. Therefore, while a model of conservation being principally philanthropic has served us to the best of its ability, we need to reinvent the concept of conservation and the institutions that deliver it.

XR has no doubt ruffled government and the establishment, as new legislation is being developed to curb the right to protest. However, as I write, several convictions of XR protestors have been overturned on appeal, on the basis that people do have the right to protest peacefully for a limited period of time, no matter whether that is blocking a road or other similar disruption, and on the basis the protests were valid in the context of climate-change legislation and commitments. Governments across the world may not have realised what creating legally binding climate targets actually have meant, and the same goes for companies and investment funds, some of whom are already facing legal action against them for continuing to cause or fund climate change. The reality is that XR is just one movement, and the level of disruption prompted by it and others will escalate beyond control if governments do not act and are seen to provide stronger, more radical leadership on the climate crisis and the wider ecological crisis.

Public disorder will also rise as people suffer the effects of these crises to a greater extent. Some societies in South Africa and South America have seen rioting and looting as a result of the pandemic, where systems have broken down and left people without basic subsistence. The consequences of climate disruption and ecosystem collapse may lead to systems collapsing on a far larger scale. The greater the inaction of global governments, the greater the threat of public disobedience and disorder.

The lack of action and protracted bureaucracy around the reintroduction of beavers is just one small example of where people have clearly taken action into their own hands and why we have mysterious populations such as the Bristol Avon beavers. We need beavers to help with the restoration of our ecosystems. Other species reintroductions are needed, too, but the keystone beavers should now be a priority.

Natural England has a code of good practice for species reintroductions, which includes landowner engagement in advance. The problem is that government departments have collectively moved too slowly on this issue. The fact that the Bristol Avon beavers have thrived unreported until now shows we can live with these creatures, and given the knowledge we have and careful planning, we can work with these efficient landscape architects to enhance and restore our environment.

Naturally, there are some concerns from people such as farmers and those invested in aquaculture about beavers returning to the UK. At Otterton, there have also been issues with dogs entering the river and attacking the beavers, with one dog coming off much worse after a mauling from the protective female. However, research shows that humans can live harmoniously with beavers if we manage the situation well.

The Cornwall Beaver Project, led by the Cornwall Wildlife Trust, is just one case that shows how beavers affect water and wildlife and how conflicts with humans can be resolved. Researchers involved visited Bavaria in Germany, where beavers have been back in residence for some 50 years, to see how the local people solved typical problems. For example, undesirable tree felling was prevented simply by sand-painting a trunk or wrapping a wire mesh around it. Unwanted floods were averted by adding a flow device to dams that allowed some water to pass through. Such simple solutions allow humans and beavers to share the same space amicably, and this is what AWT, in partnership, hopes to achieve for the Bristol Avon beavers.

The Bavarian district of Winzer has in the past faced many floods, leading to the government proposing a dam at a cost of more than a million euros. But about the same time, beavers had moved in upstream and started building their own dam. This slowed down the flow of water and reduced the impact of floods, saving the town more than 650,000 euros. This is a perfect example of how beavers can help mitigate climate-change disasters in a natural and economical way.

Contrary to popular misconception, beavers do not eat fish. In fact, ponds and channels created by these herbivores sustain fish and other freshwater species by offering habitats (including breeding and nursery grounds) and refuges during droughts. On the Bristol Avon, I have witnessed the fish nurseries created by the beavers among the mangrove-like submerged willows.

At times, beavers may be a nuisance to landowners, but they enhance the landscape and biodiversity, and limit environmental disasters in a natural, sustainable and cost-effective way. They also provide the simple joy of seeing such unique and elusive mammals, encouraging people to interact with and appreciate nature and creating new economic opportunities around wildlife and ecotourism.

9 Finding flow

Having gathered the necessary evidence of a three-generation beaver population on the Bristol Avon, I was at a bit of a loss. There wasn't the same sense of purpose now. There was still a need for data to try to monitor the spread of their activity and so model their territory and likely migration. But the possibility that the beavers were 'outed' in a way which put them at risk weighed on my mind, and I decided to pull together a montage of video footage that AWT could use to promote the beavers in a positive light and, in particular, that they had remained unnoticed for so long.

I confided in Emmy-award-winning wildlife film-maker, photographer and author Steve Nicholls and showed him some clips of the beavers to glean tips on how to make a simple amateur film. Steve was a trustee during my time at AWT and is now a friend. A visit to his house is an experience. The dining room is his wife Vicky's wildlife art studio and study for her PhD on dinosaurs, and one spare bedroom is Steve's home office, complete with film-editing screens and the largest library of natural history books I have ever seen, which spills over into the lounge. A second spare bedroom is converted into a photography studio full of tripods and insect houses. This is a house where work and life collide with passion, resulting in world-class imagery and natural history films. To live with personal interest, passion and purpose so intertwined is very special – something few people achieve.

I spent most of my limited spare time in the next week pulling out some clips for social media shorts and other media use and making a five-minute film telling the story of the Bristol Avon beavers. I also introduced AWT to Greenhouse PR, an agency I had worked with for many years, which I thought could help generate a national media story, with the positive emphasis on the Bristol beavers as a newly discovered population thriving without disturbance.

The film was a distraction, and I hadn't done any writing for a while, and I needed to find my flow again. Another minor distraction was watching Chris Packham's BBC film *The Walk That Made Me*. The walk took him along the River Itchen, near where I grew up and where I spent weekends walking our dogs with my parents. As with Chris, spotting trout, seeing swans and exploring the surrounding water meadows was a large part of my childhood. The programme instantly took me back to those days and made me want to visit again. It was particularly profound because Chris talked about walking the landscape with his father, as I had done with mine, and at the end of the programme there was a dedication to his father, who passed away just after the film was finished. One of the few pictures that I have of my own father, whom I lost a long time ago in 1995, is one I took of him sitting on the bank of the Itchen. Anticipating his own father's passing and that he would no longer be able to walk with him, Chris simply said you have to seize the day and cannot rely on tomorrow – something that I too often lose sight of.

I had already planned to be out on the river at dawn the next morning, but his words gave me back the lost sense of purpose – to live, breath and enjoy it. I had decided not to leave any more cameras out. In the high-holiday season, the risk was too great that they would be spotted and draw attention to the burrow. I set off at 4.30am as usual and was surprised how quickly the days had begun to shorten. It was roughly the same distance after the summer solstice as it was before it when I started my surveys, and it was dark. But it was considerably milder than on those early May mornings, though still a little fresh out on the river. Storm Evert had raged a few days before, swelling the river, but now all was utterly still and silent, with a feint haze rather than a full fog.

I gave a morning salute to a buzzard, kestrel and kingfisher as I made my way upriver, approaching Beaver Alley with stealth. I paddled softly, paused, listened. Nothing. I passed the burrow and was photographing the tree lying across the river – somewhat trimmed by the beavers since my last visit – when I noticed movement in the water. A beaver swam across the river on the other side of the tumbling mass of branches and disappeared behind the main trunk of the tree. Had it seen me?

I hung on the water in silence, the kayak motionless in the calm by the left-hand riverbank, looking at the large mass of fallen willow ahead. All was silent and still. Then I saw a ripple from behind the tree and realised I could hear gnawing. It is hard to describe the sound – a bit like a rasp chaffing down wood or short bursts of fingernails rubbed hard against a wooden door – but it was magical. The beaver then moved to swim around the trunk and spotted me with camera raised. It dived with a calm splash but no tail-slap. I hung on the water trying to look to my right and behind me. Suddenly I caught sight of movement in the overhang of branches on the right-hand riverbank and saw the beaver emerge and calmly surface-swim back towards the burrow. I watched it all the way, some 20 metres, before it calmly duck-dived under the sprawling willow branches that conceal the underwater entrance. It was a magical encounter made special by the beaver's calmness. The fact it saw me when I was motionless must have helped, but I like to think the beaver had realised the regular dawn visitor was a friend.

I journeyed up the river to the farthest point I could near Warleigh, collecting photo evidence of beaver activity and GPS readings and then returned to the burrow area to collect the remote cameras left on my previous survey trip. I felt some sadness not leaving out fresh ones because the discoveries made on them had given me such excitement and this felt like the end of my adventure.

I had placed one camera as close to the burrow as possible to try to get better still photographs. However, it had been triggered a lot less than before, and I wondered if this was perhaps a sign the kits were now finding their feet, or rather their webbing, and venturing away from their nursery bank. When I got home, the footage revealed a grey wagtail to be added to list of those benefiting from the beavers' landscape architecture. On another camera was a clip of a young boy lying on the front of his dad's paddleboard, waving and saying hello into the lens while, in the background, dad explained it was a wildlife camera. This proved that it had definitely been the right decision to withdraw the cameras. Footage also captured numerous canoes, kayaks and paddleboards and included a close-up of the cleavage of one young lady getting out of a canoe on the bank right in front of the camera, oblivious of it, and using the trunk it was on as balance. This footage was honourably deleted.

I spoke to both Amy and Julie in the days after the trip to advise them of the scale of river activity and confirm I'd withdrawn the cameras. We all agreed it was time for AWT to positively own the story and publicise the existence of the beavers. They also informed me that the current CEO of AWT and someone from the Beaver Trust had kayaked up to the burrow at dusk and seen the kits in evening light, quite close and intimately. Now I was free of having to put out cameras, I would have to try an evening paddle myself.

Before that, I would seize the day in other ways and get out for a dusk walk at my favourite nature reserve, Folly Farm, with Roz, to try to see deer, hare and barn owls. The hares eluded us but the others didn't disappoint, and we had several barn owl sightings and heard the barn owl chicks hissing from the nestbox. With the cameras now released from beaver duty, I couldn't resist returning the next evening to leave one trained on the box.

Most of the subsequent clips were either of branches blowing in the wind or ultra-closeups of feather ends, as the barn owl had taken a liking to using the camera on the tripod as a perch. However, there was one clip where I couldn't believe my luck. Two owlets were at the nestbox entrance, one fully out, as if waiting to fledge, and the parent had swooped into the tree canopy to feed them a vole before diving out to go back on the hunt.

Even though it was early August, I was conscious nights were already drawing in and the time to do dawn or dusk trips was closing fast. In a very mixed weather week, a window appeared when I could get out on the river at dusk, so I decided to take it just for me, free from photography and GPS recordings. It was liberating to carry no poles and the weight of various bits of kit. I had intended to take my main camera but, when I got there, realised I had forgotten to put in the memory card, which in a way was another liberation.

When I put my kayak on the river, I met a host of paddleboarders and a kayaker that must have just been either setting off for a short evening play or returning, as I didn't see any of them later. I set off on the usual three- to four-kilometre outward paddle, and as I went under the first bridge, I was passed by an early bat, which fed in the shadow of the bridge low to the water. Later, among the tightly packed trees on the bank, I caught sight of a great spotted woodpecker and watched it hop from trunk to trunk. There was a wind, but as I'd hoped, its strength faded as the sun went down, and I was able to pause on the water to watch and listen in expectation. I approached Beaver Alley silently, but there was nothing to be heard nor seen, so I pushed on. A short distance upriver my phone rang. Idiot! I'd forgotten to put it on silent. Any beaver would have taken cover now. After a brief chat with my mum, I put the phone on silent and continued upriver.

Perhaps, I thought, the beavers might still be asleep and I'd have a chance of seeing them later as I drifted back. But then I suddenly caught a glimpse of something swimming in among a tumbling willow copse. It was a kit!

I don't know why I was surprised, as my experience of badger cubs over many years is that, once they are confident and adjusted to the world, they are usually the first out of the sett, and like any growing youngster, keen to explore. The kits were clearly growing up fast. Just a few weeks ago, they were not venturing far from their riverbank crèche, being brought branches by the adults, and yet here was one, at just after 8pm, some 300 metres upriver from the burrow. I passed the willow copse and waited 100 metres upriver, supping on some chai tea from my flask and munching on a granola bar, feeling like a king. I had the calm and beauty of the river all to myself.

I drifted slowly, only occasionally dragging a paddle in the water to keep the kayak in a straight line and soon spotted shuffling in some sprigs of willow. I reached for my phone and started videoing as I drifted silently towards the shaking shoots. It was the kit some 20 metres further upriver from where we'd met, and I as drew close, it calmly turned and climbed up a branch out into the river to get a better look at me. It gently plopped into the water and then surfaced, swimming out to mid-river right in front of me before then telling me what it thought of the interruption with a still to be perfected but impressive tail-slap. It surfaced again slightly behind and left of me, but I pushed off with some soft paddle strokes to leave it in peace. I'd filmed it all and was just happy and content to have seen a kit in real life rather than just on the camera-trap clips.

Reflecting on how quickly the kits had developed and gained confidence, I realised I had been right about why the last set of camera traps had been triggered less, and I pondered the metaphor for myself – that I was wanting change and needed to push myself to find new pastures, whether that be a new home or new interests and challenges.

As I returned to Beaver Alley and the burrow area, I drifted silently again. There was no sound, no movement. Slipping past on the natural flow of the river, I inspected the burrow area. I was still looking backward at the burrow area several metres past when I realised another kit was swimming

right next to the kayak, so close I could have touched it with my paddle. I dragged a paddle to slow down and reached for my phone to film it, but before I could, the kit turned in front of the kayak to look straight at me and then dived with a clumsy *splosh*, no doubt heading back under the kayak to the tumbling willow around the burrow. It was another lovely encounter, and I headed for home feeling very lucky, collecting three beer cans, two plastic drinks bottles and piece of industrial plastic sheeting along the way.

It had been an incredible few months, getting the first pictures to prove there were beavers, then proving the river supported an established breeding population, and now getting to see the growing kits first-hand. The experience had also given me so much opportunity to reflect, to learn and, in the process, to improve both my physical and mental wellbeing. In all honesty, finding the right balance and flow remains an ongoing challenge. But through this rewarding experience, I have also rediscovered an interest in writing and formed a new relationship with a local landscape.

I made another dusk trip less than a week later, when I was presented with my final gift. I came across a yearling feeding and was able to pass it

slowly, up and then down the river on several occasions without disturbing it and to take several photographs. A few high-quality images other than those off the camera traps were the final pieces needed to support AWT's positive PR. It was also a gift to have such an intimate encounter, watching the beaver harvest willow stems, eat, dip in the river and repeat the process.

To my surprise, I also encountered a canoeist with his young son, who asked if I was out to photograph the beavers and offered that he'd heard they had kits. The secret was clearly out, which was always a risk, the more AWT partners were told about it and river-users spotted them. I somehow managed to change the subject to otters and then carried on back, this time collecting seven plastic bottles, six dog's tennis balls, three pieces of polystyrene, two beer cans, two odd flip flops and a plastic cricket ball.

As I said earlier, what I have learnt through years of wildlife encounters and adventures is that I prefer intimacy with a place – knowing somewhere,

noticing its changes and understanding its wildlife. The joy of wildlife for me is greatly enhanced when you know and anticipate where to find something and how to be around it and watch it undisturbed. Such intimacy gives a sense of connection. Living next to a coral reef where I trained to be a survey diver and then trained others taught me that. Knowing exactly where to go to find the pyjama cardinal fish or the ribbon eels is very special, as is being able to recognise through intimate knowledge and experience the out-of-place or the unusual visitor.

I would be back on the river at some point to continue the surveys for Avon Wildlife Trust, and I'd be putting out camera traps next year to see the progress of the kits and whether there was yet another new generation. But the yearling and kit encounters were a nice closure for this year, and I felt content in the knowledge they are there – that the beavers are back. Back from extinction.

Bristol Post ★★★

WEDNESDAY, SEPTEMBER 29, 2021   SOUTH WEST DAILY NEWSPAPER OF THE YEAR   InYourArea.co.uk   £1

Beavers return to Avon

RARE CREATURES RETURN TO RIVER AFTER ABSENCE OF 500 YEARS P3

INSIDE

 Sky News ✓
@SkyNews

"Build back beaver"

Boris Johnson says his government will rewild 30% of Britain, restore natural wildlife and also invest in new "beautiful" homes on brown sites.

trib.al/ie0FUMu

 PM SPEECH

Scan this QR code with your phone for instant reaction on the Sky News live blog

BUILD BACK BETTER

🔴 LIVE   Manchester

NEWS

Home | Coronavirus | Climate | UK | World | Business | Politics | Tech | Science | Health | Family & Education

England | Local News | Regions | Bristol

River Avon wild beaver family sighting 'extremely significant'

🕒 29 September

It's the first time wild beavers have been seen living in the area without human intervention for more than 400 years

Postscript

As the September nights were drawing in and the dusk light fading, I made one last evening trip to the river. I took my friend Dominic with me, and we had a wonderful encounter with a kit swimming towards us and passing by Dom's kayak close to the river bank. We were not, however, the only ones out hoping to spot the beavers, so word was clearly out among the paddleboarding and local community.

Then on 28 September, I was tipped off by AWT that a press release on the beavers had been issued, embargoed for the following day. I woke early, and checking the news, I could see that the beavers already had national and Southwest regional coverage. By mid-morning the beavers were covered in 232 online articles or posts, and the numbers continued to grow. All of the coverage I saw was positive and served to raise awareness of their importance and potential return to the landscape.

Major coverage included the news bulletin on BBC Radio 4's *Today* programme, both the BBC News and ITV News websites, many of the national newspapers, including the *Daily Mail*, *Metro* and *Evening Standard*, the BBC's regional *Points West* television news, Radio Bristol and countless regional newspapers, as it was syndicated by the Press Association. Several outlets used film clips of the beaver family, which drew attention. At one time the story was trending and made the top stories on the *BBC News* homepage. A friend sent a text message to tell me, but I was on an away-day at Folly Farm with my team and had no TV and intermittent connectivity, and so ironically I missed most of the coverage. The beavers even looked back at tens of thousands of people from news-stands across Bristol as they made the front cover of the *Bristol Post*.

Catching up with it all the next day was extraordinary, and Amy had done some great interviews including one where she is used as the voiceover to clips of the beavers playing, feeding and grooming. She landed lots of great messages, promoting the role of the beaver and giving insights to the public on their behaviour and the signs to look out for. The online coverage also reputedly reached the US, Canada and even as far as Australia. As an awareness exercise implanting the importance of the beavers' return into people's consciousness, it was a huge success, which drove interest in the Trust's website and fundraising appeals.

My brief foray with being a widely published wildlife photographer was surreal. Just when I thought it couldn't get more so, a week later, Prime Minister Boris Johnson mentioned the beavers in his speech at the annual Conservative Party conference:

"… We are going to rewild parts of the country and consecrate a total of 30% to nature. We're planting tens of millions of trees. Otters are returning to rivers from which they've been absent for decades, beavers that have not been seen on some rivers since Tudor times, massacred for their pelts, are now back. And if that isn't conservatism, my friends, I don't know what is. Build back beaver, I say. Build back beaver. Though the beavers may sometimes build without local authority permission, you can also see how much room there is to build the homes that young families need in this country. Not on green fields, not just jammed in the Southeast, but beautiful homes on brownfield sites in places where homes make sense."

The term 'Build back beaver' was widely quoted in the media and online, largely speculating what on earth it meant, and several people I spoke to were rather irritated that latching onto the beavers' story was being used as an example of nature's restoration in order to justify more house building.

I was similarly disheartened, but on reflection, I realised that, firstly, it showed the impact of the media coverage – that even the Prime Minister was aware of 'wild and free' beavers living without conflict with people – and, secondly, that the pledge to 'Build Back Beaver' is something to hold the government to account on. If further obstacles and delays in reintroducing beavers continued, then there would be plenty of people ready to remind the Prime Minister and his government of his pledge.

The Times ran an article entitled 'Here's how we build back beaver', and Times Radio even polled the popularity of beavers among the British public, with nearly half (45 per cent) saying they like or love beavers and only 9 per cent saying they either dislike or hate them. The remaining 46 per cent didn't have strong opinions either way.

The extent of the media coverage meant Natural England decided to include beavers in its national surveys in 2022, meaning they will be officially recognised and benefit from any future protections. AWT has managed to fund a project officer to engage local landowners and others who could be affected by beavers. Initial conversations have already shown that beavers have indeed been present on the By Brook for some time but not widely disclosed, adding further evidence that we can live in harmony with them.

Since this book was first published, the government introduced new legislation that classifies beavers as a native species again, which affords them protection and legalises wider releases and spread. We still need to ensure that supporting their protection is properly resourced. My own action to learn more about beavers carries on, and while reading about the Beaver Trust, I was intrigued to find reference to the Bevis Trust – named after the same book I was named after – which cares for 300 acres in Carmarthenshire with a rewilding focus and is home to four captive families of beavers. The coincidence is scarcely believable, but I now know where at least one of my wildlife trips will be to next year. Bevis visiting beavers at the Bevis Trust – I can't wait.

Build back beaver, I say!

Acknowledgements

I feel hugely privileged to have had the opportunity to discover and intimately experience a wild and free beaver family. I shall forever be indebted to Amy Coulthard and Julie Doherty from the Avon Wildlife Trust for entrusting me with the task to collect evidence on their existence.

Many thanks to Roz Kidman Cox and Simon Bishop for their skill, support and patience with this book project, and to all those mentioned in the book who have been part of this journey.

Thank you to Triodos Bank for the image in the prologue, taken at the March 2020 Greta Thunberg-led Fridays for Future school-strike climate march in Bristol, and to my colleagues Ellie James and Ellen Harrison, who are marching either side of me.

Thank you also to Owen Newman for the use of his image on the opening page of Chapter 8, taken in September 2018 at the People's Walk for Wildlife march in London, and to Angela Julian for her image of the walk on page 123.

I am also very grateful to Greenhouse PR, which I have worked with for nearly 15 years and which provided considerable pro-bono support to promote the positive return of wild, free and breeding beavers to our landscape.

References

The Eurasian Beaver Handbook: Ecology and management of Castor fiber.
By Róisín Campbell-Palmer et al. Pelagic Publishing.

Bringing Back the Beaver: The story of one man's quest to rewild Britain's waterways. By Derek Gow. Chelsea Green Publishing.

Nature's Architect: The beaver's return to our wild landscapes.
By Jim Crumley. Saraband.

Eager: The Surprising, Secret Life of Beavers and Why They Matter.
By Ben Goldfarb. Chelsea Green Publishing.

Nature's Home magazine, winter/spring 2021. RSPB.

Avon Wildlife Trust www.avonwildlifetrust.org.uk/beavers

Devon Wildlife Trust www.devonwildlifetrust.org/what-we-do/beavers

The Beaver Trust https://beavertrust.org

The Bevis Trust www.bevistrust.com

Author

Dubbed by the media as the first environmentalist to run a bank, **Bevis Watts** has spent 25 years working and volunteering in sustainability, with a career that has included environmental research, recycling, conservation and banking. He is currently Chief Executive of Triodos Bank UK.